Ten By Ten Book One

Ten Ten-Minute Plays

Kenneth P. Langer

Brass Bell Books and Games

BRASS BELL
BOOKS & GAMES

Contents

Performance

To pubicly perform any of these plays,
please contact the author:
Kenneth Langer (klangerdude@gmail.com)

Introduction

[At flipping of the page, the author and a devoted reader sit facing each other in any kind of setting you like. Behind them stands a strange person who does not move.]

READER: What's a ten-minute play?

AUTHOR: Seriously?

READER: It seemed like the best question to start with.

AUTHOR: OK, fine. It's a play that last ten minutes long.

READER: That's it? No special literary requirements? Maybe it has to rhyme a certain way or the lines have to be a specific number of words or you have to use an egg timer while you read it. You know, something like that.

AUTHOR: Nope. The only requirement is that the play should last about ten minutes in length.

READER: Any kind of play?

AUTHOR: Yes.

READER: Comedy?

AUTHOR: Yes.

READER: Tragedy?

AUTHOR: Yes.

READER: Tragicomedy?

AUTHOR: Yes, yes.

READER: Comically tragic melodrama?

AUTHOR: You can stop now.

READER: Historically autobiographical melodramatic musical? Sorry, I was on a roll. (*a beat*) So why would anyone want to write a play that only lasts ten minutes?

AUTHOR: Well, for one thing, in our modern world of fast-paced communication, people have developed rather short...

READER: I'm sorry. Were you saying something?

AUTHOR: I was saying that people tend to lose their focus when they don't feel engaged.

READER: Oh, please. You're not going to go into that droll discussion about how social media has created an epidemic of short attention spans, are you?

AUTHOR: Well, I, uh, guess not.

READER: Good. I can't take yet another lecture about how we are not interacting... Hang on, I think I have a call coming in... Nope. It was just the timer on my phone. Well, thank you so much for this fascinating discussion but I...

AUTHOR: The interview's over already?

READER: What? You haven't talked enough about yourself yet?

AUTHOR: But you asked me why anyone would write a ten minute play.

READER: Oh, right. Go ahead but, just move it along a little, would you? (*looks uncomfortably at the strange person standing nearby*)

AUTHOR: Well, to begin with, writing a very short play is an interesting challenge for a writer. Within the span of ten minutes you have to create believable characters and interesting scenes and then put those things into a story that has an engaging and unique beginning, middle, and end.

READER: And you wanted to take on that challenge?

AUTHOR: Precisely.

READER: Well, good to know. Thank you very much for...

AUTHOR: You know, a lot of authors write ten minute plays as a way of developing their skill as writers of full-length plays. They may see them as writing exercises.

READER: I take it you don't see it that way.

AUTHOR: That's right. I've always enjoyed more concise works of art: piano preludes, poetry, models, mini-wheats.

READER: Because?

AUTHOR: Because everything is important. There's no fluff, no stalling. Every detail has to relate to the story.

READER: Every detail?

AUTHOR: Yes. Every single word.

READER: No extra material?

AUTHOR: Nope!

READER: None?

AUTHOR: None!

READER: Zero?

AUTHOR: Zip!

READER: Zilch?

AUTHOR: Nada!

READER: (*a beat*) Would you look over the garbage you just wrote?

AUTHOR: Not garbage. (*looks into the distance*) Existential meanderings through the limitless possibilities of space and time.

READER: Huh?

AUTHOR: Another feature of ten minute plays that I find interesting: the ability to be experimental. Short plays allow you to try new and different things that longer plays might not ever be able to pull off and it allows writers to explore a lot of different possibilities.

READER: So you can actually do quite a lot in a short period of time?

AUTHOR: That's right.

READER: It also keeps writers from going on and on and on.
AUTHOR: Well, uh...

READER: There's no lengthy drawn-out psychological unfoldings of their own deep-seated personal and social issues spewed out over a copious amount of paper for their own gratification?

AUTHOR: I guess you could say...

READER: And no verbose wearisome tirades about personal inadequacies projected onto a slew of character representations with developmental issues?

AUTHOR: Uh, that sounds about right.

READER: Did you have anything more to add?

AUTHOR: Um... no.

READER: OK, then. Good talk.

>   *[READER starts to exit but bumps into the STRANGE PERSON who has been standing there the entire time.]*

READER: Oh, pardon me.

STRANGE PERSON: No problem.

READER: Looking for something?

STRANGE PERSON: I'm waiting for Beckett.

READER: I see. Well, good luck with that.

CURTAIN

Synopses

Couple Seeking Conflict – A Comedy

Two characters discuss their boring lives and decide they need some conflict to make things interesting. Before nearly getting into a fight about their situation, they finally agree on a scenario that pits them against each other and they prepare to put their scheme into action.

The Insurance Salesman – A Dark Comedy

An insurance salesperson reaches out to a potential client. What he is selling, though, is not life insurance but death insurance. It's a different piece of mind.

Moonwalk – A Comedy

Two astronauts leave their spaceship to walk on the surface of the moon. They are assigned to fix some machinery but one of them decides to explore and finds a strange object that directly affects both of them.

Green Grows The Garden – A Drama

Two detectives question a suspect accused of starting a fire near a homeless shelter. Though he has confessed to the crime, the detectives believe he is holding back on the truth.

The Shootout – A Comedy

Two gunfighters agree to a duel to settle their families' age-old feud but playing by the rules was never for either gunslinger and the resulting showdown goes terribly awry.

Dinner at Dinah's – A Comedy

Between shows, a couple members of the audience cause a disturbance that reveals their own insecurities.

Find The Mole – A Comedy

Two spies come together for a secret meeting in the hopes of rooting out a mole in their clandestine organization.

We Three – A Christmas Comedy

Three unusual people come together to discuss the trials and tribulations of trying to save the world one nightmare at a time.

An Inconvenient Crime – A Comedy

A stranger asks a couple at their home if he could possibly rob them that evening–only if it is convenient–but it could all be part of a bigger plot.

The Waiting Room – A Drama

A father waits patiently for his family to return because it's the only thing he can do.

Couple Seeking Conflict

<u>Characters</u>

(2A)

CHARACTER 1 (M or F) - A character in an upcoming but not yet written play.

CHARACTER 2 (M or F) - Another character in the same unwritten play.

Note: The Characters can be of any gender or ethnicity. Gender-specific language can be changed as needed.

<u>Scene</u>

An empty stage with a table and two chairs.

<u>Time</u>

Present.

[At rise, CHARACTER 1 is sitting on a chair near the table reading a paper or maybe a device with the news. CHARACTER 2 enters and sees CHARACTER 1.]

CHARACTER 2: Hey!

CHARACTER 1: *(does not look up)* Hey!

CHARACTER 2: How's it going?

CHARACTER 1: Fine… Just fine.

CHARACTER 2: Good, good! *(sits down)* So, how are you?

CHARACTER 1: *(puts down the paper)* Me? Oh, I'm good.

CHARACTER 2: Oh, great, great.

CHARACTER 1: Yeah, you?

CHARACTER 2: Oh, no complaints.

CHARACTER 1: Oh well, that's good.

CHARACTER 2: (*pauses, looks away, then looks back*) The family?

CHARACTER 1: Oh, yeah. Fine. Everyone's fine.

CHARACTER 2: Oh, good. Glad to hear it. (*pause*) House?

CHARACTER 1: House is good. No problems. (*pause*) Except for...

CHARACTER 2: (*suddenly excited*) Yes?

CHARACTER 1: Oh no, I forgot. We got that fixed last week.

CHARACTER 2: (*disappointed*) Oh, well. That's good.

CHARACTER 1: Yup. Good.

CHARACTER 2: (*pause*) Kids?

CHARACTER 1: Great.

CHARACTER 2: Job?

CHARACTER 1: Couldn't be happier.

CHARACTER 2: (*pause, then with anticipation*) In-laws?

CHARACTER 1: No problem.

CHARACTER 2: (*Disappointed*) What? You get along with your in-laws?

CHARACTER 1: They're away on vacation... somewhere in the Bahamas... couldn't be happier.

CHARACTER 2: Oh, how nice for you.

CHARACTER 1: (*pause*) Why? (*with anticipation*) You having problems?

CHARACTER 2: With what?

CHARACTER 1: YOUR in-laws?

CHARACTER 2: Umm... (*thinks for a moment*) Oh, no, no. They're very nice people.

CHARACTER 1: (*unconvincingly*) Well, that's very nice for you. (*picks up the paper again*)

CHARACTER 2: Yes... yes it is. (*pause*) How about your, uh, dog?

CHARACTER 1: Dog?

CHARACTER 2: Yeah. How's that great little pup of yours? I know how much it means to you.

CHARACTER 1: No dog.

CHARACTER 2: (*suddenly animated*) What? Oh no! I'm so sorry. Oh, this must just be terrible for you. What horrible news! What happened?

CHARACTER 1: (*looks at CHARACTER 2*) Never had a dog.

CHARACTER 2: What? No dog? I could have sworn you told me you just got a new...

CHARACTER 1: Nope.

CHARACTER 2: Oh, how sad for you. You should really get a dog.

CHARACTER 1: Got a cat.

CHARACTER 2: Oh? How's the...

CHARACTER 1: Fine.

CHARACTER 2: Oh.

CHARACTER 1: And a goldfish.

CHARACTER 2: Oh! A pet fish? A pet fish, you say. Well, you must know what kind of challenges come with owning a pet fish. They're so delicate, those little fishies. One minute they're fine, swimming around in their little bowls with the snapping clam and the scuba diver with air bubbles coming out of his head and then... wham! The tiny tropical aquatic member of your close-knit family is sick with some growth on its side or is swimming backward with a sorrowful look on its miniature face saying 'help me, help me.'

CHARACTER 1: (*looks at CHARACTER 1 with disdain*) The fish is fine, thank you.

CHARACTER 2: Oh, yeah, sure. Now it is. Just wait until you get back home.

CHARACTER 1: Look! Everything is just fine, hunky-dory, A-OK. (*pause*) You?

CHARACTER 2: Huh?

CHARACTER 1: House, family, car, pets, neighbors, children, annoying insects, rashes, allergies... anything? Anything at all amiss, off-kilter, disrupting your life?

CHARACTER 2: Umm... (*thinks*) Nope!

CHARACTER 1: Ugh! (*puts down the paper*) You see? That's the problem, isn't it?

CHARACTER 2: It is?

CHARACTER 1: Yes, precisely.

CHARACTER 2: I, uh, don't follow.

CHARACTER 1: There's no conflict here. We're just two characters in a play with nothing happening.

CHARACTER 2: You mean we can't just have nice peaceful lives?

CHARACTER 1: Who wants to see that?

CHARACTER 2: Maybe it could be a play about two nice guys who share their happy stories together.

CHARACTER 1: (*a beat*) You're kidding, right?

CHARACTER 2: No. Maybe it would be a good change, something refreshing.

CHARACTER 1: Refreshing? Like a cold shower or biting into a bowl of mints. (*a beat*) You see this? (*holds up the paper and flips some pages*) Murder, corruption, disaster. It's wall to wall conflict and people devour it like they do their buttered bagels and frosted croissants. Every morning pain and sorrow is delivered neatly and promptly onto their doorsteps or devices.

CHARACTER 2: Surely there must be some good news.

CHARACTER 1: You mean like the rescue worker who dives heedlessly into the fire disregarding his or her own personal safety in order to rescue a helpless child?

CHARACTER 2: Yeah. People want to hear about that too.

CHARACTER 1: Do they really? Somebody reads that and thinks, 'oh that's wonderful. What a great thing but how does that make me look? What have I done to save anyone? My life is so useless.' But, when they see all the horror they can say 'but look, I am safe and my life is so much better than the rest of the world.'

CHARACTER 2: Now that's just plain cynical.

CHARACTER 1: Is it? Come here and see for yourself. (*takes Character 2 by the arm downstage to the edge of the stage*) Look out there. (*points to the audience*) What do you see?

CHARACTER 2: A bunch of people.

CHARACTER 1: And what do they want?

CHARACTER 2: Intellectually stimulating discourse?

> [*CHARACTER 1 should feel free to improvise the next lines*]

CHARACTER 1: No! Conflict! Here look at this one. (*points to a member of the audience*) Bored to tears. Trying to keep his eyes open just so his wife won't get mad at him but secretly wishes he was on the back nine with a cigar while he talks stock options. And her! (*points to another member of the audience*) She's biding her time by imagining how the stage might look as a dance floor for a rave party. They don't want pleasantries. They want an epic struggle that breaks down our false personas and shatters the banality of our existence.

CHARACTER 1: They want all that?

CHARACTER 2: And more, because it helps them temporarily break away from the meaningless monotony that is their lives. They're waiting for the conflict and it's our job as characters to give it to them. (*returns to seat*)

CHARACTER 2: (*waves to the audience* then *returns to seat*) OK, then. How do we give them some good old fashioned conflict?

CHARACTER 1: Simple. We just think of a problem, something that threatens the definition of who we are or what we believe, something that brings us to the brink of destruction.

CHARACTER 2: That sounds terrible.

CHARACTER 1: That's kind of the point. (*stares intently at CHARACTER 2*) Are you sure you're up for this?

CHARACTER 2: What? What do you mean?

CHARACTER 1: I'm not sure you have what it takes for this kind of intense work.

CHARACTER 2: What exactly do you mean? I can do conflict as well as anyone else.

CHARACTER 1: Really? When's the last time you stood up for yourself? I bet you haven't been in a truly nasty argument since childhood.

CHARACTER 2: Oh yeah? I was very nearly in a fight just the other day.

CHARACTER 1: Very nearly?

CHARACTER 2: Yeah. I was walking down the street minding my own business when this guy bumps into me. Doesn't even say he's sorry–just keeps walking–like he's some kind of special somebody and I think to myself 'I should give that guy a piece of my mind and tell him what kind of rude person he is and if he doesn't listen, I should just pop him in the nose.'

CHARACTER 1: That's what you were thinking, huh? And when you were done thinking, what did you do next?

CHARACTER 2: I, uh, watched him chase some other guy down the street. (*a beat*) I think I waved.

CHARACTER 1: This is never going to work! You're too inexperienced. How are we going to have a conflict if you're not willing to stand up for yourself?

CHARACTER 2: It was a cop chasing a bad guy. What was I supposed to do?

CHARACTER 1: The point is you never do anything to defend yourself or anyone else, for that matter. Your whole life is a loosely strung series of abandoned and surrendered opportunities.

CHARACTER 2: How would you know anything about my life? What gives you the right to judge me?

CHARACTER 1: You do, because you stand for nothing. You're not even willing to stand up for yourself. Right now you're contemplating any way you can to just leave–thinking that if you do, you will demonstrate what a better person you are when, in reality, all you will be doing is demonstrating your cowardliness.

CHARACTER 2: Is that so? (*stands*) Well, I'll have you know I'm not afraid of you. You're just a two-dimensional character peppered with the stock traits of a bully.

CHARACTER 1: (*stands*) Oh, such clever words, but they cannot mask a lifetime of escape and withdrawal from important issues and defining moments that should have shaped you into becoming a great leading role but now you are no more than a bit part.

CHARACTER 2: Why you!

[*CHARACTER 2 rushes over to CHARACTER 1 and*

grabs a collar or shoulder with one hand while making a fist and rearing it back with the other. But before throwing a punch, suddenly freezes and stares at CHARACTER 1]

CHARACTER 2: Oh, oh, oh. You! You're really good!

CHARACTER 1: Yeah?

CHARACTER 2: Oh yeah. You had me going... you really had me going. I wanted to clean your clock there for a second. (*releases CHARACTER 2*)

CHARACTER 1: But wasn't it exhilarating, even for just a moment? Did you feel the rush, the excitement as we inched closer to the brink?

CHARACTER 2: (*sits and thinks*) Yeah... yeah, I did.

CHARACTER 1: (*sits*) The power of conflict!

CHARACTER 2: So, what we need is a situation that brings us to that point of intersection.

CHARACTER 1: Right, the place where our wills and our desires are forced to crash against each other like when the sea slams against the cliff.

CHARACTER 2: Like, say I lost my job.

CHARACTER 1: A terrible event, no doubt, but we need more. (*thinks*) How's this? I stole your job.

CHARACTER 2: You're such a cold-hearted character. (*thinks*) OK. I decide to go to my former boss and plead my case to get my old job back.

CHARACTER 1: Yes, yes. (*thinks*) But I decide to hijack your efforts so I go to the boss and reveal some kind of false but terrible rumor about you.

CHARACTER 2: Oh? What would that be?

CHARACTER 1: That you were a convicted criminal.

CHARACTER 2: Vicious! (*a beat*) I'll just deny it.

CHARACTER 1: Ah, but you see the beauty of some rumors is that they are hard to dismiss. While you are busy denying it, your boss will be thinking, 'but *he* might be a convicted criminal. How do I know I can trust *him*?'

CHARACTER 2: So the boss denies me the opportunity to get my job back.

CHARACTER 1: Dismisses it as some kind of pressure from higher up, something about efficiency graphs and the like.

CHARACTER 2: And on my way out I am feeling dejected and angry. I see you there... at my old desk... holding my old stapler.

CHARACTER 1: And I'm smiling... A wide nasty smile. But, what do you do? You could confront me directly or you could silently pass me by as you concoct a dastardly way to get even with me. (*a beat*) the stage is set for conflict.

CHARACTER 2: Yeah, conflict. (*a beat*) So, how do we get started?

CHARACTER 1: We can't.

CHARACTER 2: What? We can't? Why not?

CHARACTER 1: Because we're out of time.

CHARACTER 2: Out of time? Oh! That's a problem.

> *[The lights fade out as CHARACTER 1 picks up the paper and CHARACTER 2 stares into the distance.]*

> <u>Curtain</u>

The Insurance Salesman

[At rise, Ms. ABEL is seated behind the desk looking over a file and making notes. After a few moments, Mrs. DONOVAN enters and approaches the desk.]

DONOVAN: Are you Ms. Abel?

ABEL: (*extends her hand*) Patricia Abel of Ubiti Insurance. You must be Mrs. Donovan.

DONOVAN: Yes I am. (*shakes her hand*)

ABEL: Please, have a seat, Mrs. Donovan. I was just reviewing your file.

DONOVAN: (*sits*) Ubiti Insurance Company. That's a rather unusual name.

ABEL: (*sits*) Our founder was not from here..

DONOVAN: Oh, I see.

ABEL: Did you have any trouble finding us?

DONOVAN: (*looks around*) I have to say your office is a little bit off the beaten path and, uh, sparse.

ABEL: It's all part of our company philosophy. We're not one of those insurance companies with the skyscraper downtown and the thick glass windows that allow their executives to lord over the people of the city. We strive to keep our costs down and pass the savings on to our customers.

DONOVAN: Well, I can appreciate that.

ABEL: Yes, well, we are less worried about our image and more concerned with the well being of the people we help. (*a beat*) Speaking of which, how can I help you, Mrs. Donovan?

DONOVAN: Well, it was my husband who sent me. He said I needed some additional insurance.

ABEL: Sounds like a smart idea.

DONOVAN: He said that his cousin's family in... um, uh... Tallahassee was very happy with the program. He said they were taken care of nicely when his cousin died but (*a beat*) I'm confused. We already have life insurance. Why would we need more from another company?

ABEL: Well, you see, Mrs. Donovan, no insurance policy on its own can cover all possibilities. In fact, many of their policies are designed to be insufficient.

DONOVAN: Insufficient? I don't understand.

ABEL: It's a great irony of the insurance business that they are all more than willing to take your money but are not so eager to pay it out to your family after you die. The more ways they can figure out not to pay their clients, the more money they have to pay for those lavish office buildings.

DONOVAN: They're all just a bunch of snakes if you ask me. (*a beat*) No offense to you.

ABEL: Oh, none taken. I completely understand. It's part of why we are here.

DONOVAN: But you're one of them.

ABEL: One of who?

DONOVAN: One of those life insurance agents.

ABEL: Oh, Mrs. Donovan. I'm afraid your husband didn't explain the situation to you at all. We are not a life insurance agency, we are a death insurance agency.

DONOVAN: A death insurance agency?

ABEL: Yes. We take care of all the things that a life insurance company does not.

DONOVAN: Oh?

ABEL: Let me ask you a question, Mrs. Donovan. What is it that you most fear about this time of your life?

DONOVAN: Well, I don't fear death, if that's what you mean, but what I do fear is the dying.

ABEL: The pain, the suffering, the long drawn-out stay in a hospital, the loss of precious memories, and, worst of all, the burden that you may be on your family.

DONOVAN: (*whispers*) Yes!

ABEL: Life insurance does nothing to help you with any of these worries. All those companies care about is that you stay alive as long as you can so that someone will pay the premiums and then they hope you off yourself so they won't have to pay out anything to your family due to some suicide clause.

DONOVAN: But that's not what you do?

ABEL: No. When the time comes we take care of you. You would be sent away someplace where you can be comfortable and looked after while your family gets the life insurance money they deserve and need to carry on with their lives. We make sure that everyone thinks you have died a death that cannot be questioned.

DONOVAN: You would take care of me?

ABEL: Absolutely. We will put you up in very comfortable and peaceful surroundings. All your meals and needs are taken care of. We will see to it that you will feel no pain and that your mind is at ease all while your family is also taken care of.

DONOVAN: But how can you do that?

ABEL: We have a company filled with very dedicated employees.

DONOVAN: I'll say! What more could a person hope for?

ABEL: Precisely.

DONOVAN: (*thinks for a moment*) You said, 'when the time comes.' What does that mean?

ABEL: Well, you designate someone as your primary caretaker. I would presume that person might be your husband?

DONOVAN: Yes.

ABEL: Well, then, that person would trigger something we call 'The Event.' When this happens the client–possibly you–is taken to the place of refuge. The family says their goodbyes and are sworn to secrecy. In the meantime, the current life insurance company is informed that the client died in a manner that does not trigger any investigations or reviews. The family gets the full amount of their policy and the client gets a long lasting piece of mind.

DONOVAN: It all sounds so wonderful. My husband's mother... uh, Sarah, no, uh... Susan. Yes, Susan got Alzheimer's and spent years slowly slipping away while her family had to do more and more for her. It must have been horrible.

ABEL: Do you need some time to think about it? (*reaches for some papers*) I can leave you with some brochures and we can make another appointment.

DONOVAN: Well, I, uh...

ABEL: No, really. You need to take your time making such an important decision. There is a lot to think about, a lot to consider. (*a beat*) Just don't take too long. A terrible illness or life-threatening accident can happen at any moment. We're all living on borrowed time and need to make the decisions that will guide us along the least treacherous path. Who knows what might happen to you the moment you walk out that door? Heart attack? Stroke? It's unpleasant to think about these things I know but sometimes we must. But... you take your time. (*pulls out a datebook or device*) Shall we schedule a follow-up?

DONOVAN: (*after a moment*) No, no. I don't need any additional time. I've made up my mind. I want to do what's best for my family.

ABEL: Of course you do, Mrs. Donovan. Of course you do. Are you ready to begin, then?

DONOVAN: Yes.

ABEL: It's really just a matter of some paperwork.

> [*ABEL produces a giant stack of paperwork and slides it all in front of DONOVAN.*]

ABEL: This is the complete prospectus that explains every detail of the services we provide and all their variations. When you're done going through them I can show you the contracts and discuss your options.

> [*DONOVAN stares at the stack of papers but does not move.*]

ABEL: Well, I guess it is a little overwhelming, isn't it? I tell you what. You have been so nice and honest with me. Let's make this easy. (*pulls out a thin folder*) Why don't I just show you the standard option? No bells and whistles, just the coverage and assurance you are seeking. (*opens the folder*) All you need to do is sign these few papers and you can be on your way with an easy mind.

DONOVAN: (*sighs*) Ah, well thank you, Ms. Abel. I so hate all that legal mumbo-jumbo.

ABEL: I completely understand, Mrs. Donovan. You are a busy person and have better things to do than sit around in some dank office reading mind-numbing documents.

DONOVAN: Thank you for understanding.

ABEL: Shall we begin, then?

DONOVAN: Yes.

ABEL: Fine.

> *[ABEL pulls out some papers from the folder. She hands each one to DONOVAN who then signs them.]*

ABEL: This is the contract that names you as the client... This is the contract that allows you to name someone as your caretaker. As you see here (*points*) we have taken the liberty of putting your husband's name here. You sign here... This paper allows us to work directly with your current life insurance program... this document covers the details concerning The Event... and this final contract covers any miscellaneous problems that may arise during the transition phase... This here lists the fees.

DONOVAN: (*looks at the paper*) Oh my! That's a lot of money.

ABEL: Keep in mind this is the basic option, not the silver or gold packages. We have kept the costs at a minimum but there are legal fees and all the costs involved with your needs.

DONOVAN: What does the silver option include?

ABEL: Oh, just trinkets and filigree for those concerned with appearances. Would you like to see the proposal?

DONOVAN: Oh, no. I'm happy with the basic option. (*she signs the paper*)

ABEL: That's it. You're done.

DONOVAN: Oh, well. That was easy.

ABEL: Nothing to it. (*shakes her hand*) You are another proud client of the Ubiti Insurance Company. Do you have any final questions?

DONOVAN: Oh, no. I think you have covered everything.

ABEL: Great! I'm glad to have been of service to you.

> [*ABEL reaches for her briefcase and puts it up on her desk. She begins to stuff papers into it including the signed contracts.*]

ABEL: Well, if you'll excuse me, I have to get to my next appointment. I have to meet a client at the out of town office.

DONOVAN: I thought this was your office.

ABEL: Oh, well, we have several satellite offices situated around town so that we can be available to everyone.

DONOVAN: Oh, I see. (*thinks for a moment*) Um, I do have one more question.

ABEL: (*stops moving papers*) Of course, what can I tell you?

DONOVAN: This Event thing that you talked about?

ABEL: Yes?

DONOVAN: How will I know when it happens? I mean, will my husband just tell me or does it have to be some kind of secret thing?

ABEL: Oh, Mrs. Donovan, you don't need to worry about any of that!

DONOVAN: What? Why?

ABEL: Your husband has already triggered it.

DONOVAN: What? I don't understand. I'm fine. I mean, yeah, I forget things sometimes but who doesn't? I know I've neglected to eat a meal once in a while or to take a shower regularly but that doesn't mean anything. I'm not ready to transition yet.

> *[ABEL reaches into her briefcase and pulls out a gun. She shoots DONOVAN then puts the gun away. DONOVAN falls to the floor.]*

ABEL: No one ever is.

> *[ABEL picks up her briefcase and turns to exit the stage. Her last line is spoken just before she exits or offstage.]*

ABEL: Clean up in room three!

<u>Curtain</u>

Moonwalk

Cast (3A)

JOE: Call sign Eagle One. An astronaut on the surface of the moon or a planet. Wears a space suit. Very curious and lighthearted.

TOM: Call sign Eagle Two. Another astronaut on the surface of the moon or a planet. Wears a space suit. Very professional but likes to have fun.

HOUSTON: The communications officer back on earth.

Note: The Characters can be of any gender or ethnicity. Changes in gender-specific words can be made where needed.

Scene

The majority of the center and upstage is the surface of the moon or a planet as seen through a video feed. The effect is created not so much by the stage or props but through the actions and words of the two actors portraying the astronauts. Their movements should be slow and bouncy as if walking in a low gravity environment. Their words should be spoken slowly and can sometimes be clipped as if the feed is temporarily interrupted. They may even make occasional jerky movements or add garbled sounds.

Downstage and to the stage right side is a table and a chair facing upstage. Various props can be put on the table to make it look more like an electronic communications station but are not necessary.

The side curtains should be black and should be visible slightly to the audience.

Time

The present or possibly a near future when further space exploration is possible.

> [*At rise, HOUSTON is seated at a table facing upstage.*]

HOUSTON: Eagle One, this is Houston. Do you read? (*pause*) I say again, Eagle One. Do you copy? This is Mission Control.

> [*JOE enters from stage left. He moves in slow with a bouncing motion as if on the surface of a low gravity planet.*]

JOE: Copy Houston. I read you five by five.

HOUSTON: Very good, Joe. Can you give me a status update?

JOE: Roger that. Temperature is good. Suit seems fine. Oxygen levels at 81%. Shouldn't have had that dehydrated chili though.

HOUSTON: Feeling a little pressure in that lower compartment, Eagle One?

JOE: That's a roger, Roger.

HOUSTON: Roger, Roger?

JOE: Isn't your name Roger?

HOUSTON: No. It's Reginald

JOE: Reginald?

HOUSTON: Yes, Reginald. (*a beat*) Could I get an update on the mission, please?

JOE: Roger, Reggie, we're ready steady.

HOUSTON: Could we stick to protocol, please?

JOE: (*a little woozy*) I read you loud and clear, Houston. Stand by... I am en route to the radar array to make adjustments as defined in the, uh, you know, mission thing.

HOUSTON: I copy.

JOE: And I copy.

HOUSTON: Repeat your last transmission, Eagle One. I'm not sure I received it correctly.

JOE: I said I copy

HOUSTON: You copy what?

JOE: I copy your copy which would make me a carbon copy, copy?

HOUSTON: (*a pause*) Eagle One, would you please check the O2/CO2 flow in your suit? We think the mixture may be off.

> [*JOE makes a hissing sound as he changes something on his suit.*]

JOE: (*regains his composure*) External gas mixture adjusted.

HOUSTON: Copy that, Eagle One. Feel better?

JOE: That's a roger... I mean yes. Sorry about the confusion. Mission is still a go. Reaching radar array now.

> [*JOE moves to a real or imagined device and begins working on it.*]

HOUSTON: Eagle One, be advised. We have signs of intense solar winds on way to your position.

JOE: So advised, Houston. (*a beat*) Could you read out those adjustment specs for the polarization?

HOUSTON: Copy, Joe. We need a 2.3% angle rotation on the microwave.

JOE: Copy 2.3% angle adjustment. Stand by... Houston, I'm going to need the next size calibration wrench. Stand by.

HOUSTON: Mission Control standing by.

JOE: Eagle One to Eagle Two. Do you read?

TOM: (*offstage*) This is Eagle Two. I copy. Nearly suited up. What is it, Joe? You forget which way to turn the wrench?

JOE: I need the number 4 calibration wrench. I only brought numbers one to three.

TOM: Yours not big enough?

JOE: I tried to sweet-talk it but it doesn't seem to want to give it up.

TOM: Ain't that always the way?

> *[TOM crosses from stage left towards JOE moving in the same slow and bouncy low-gravity manner. Just before he gets there, both TOM and JOE act is if they are knocked over by a sudden blast of wind.]*

TOM and JOE: Whoa!

TOM: (*struggling to get up*) What was that?

JOE: High solar winds.

TOM: And very little gravity to hold us... Here you go. (*hands JOE the wrench*)

HOUSTON: Eagle Two, this is Mission Control. What's your status?

TOM: (*checks his suit*). Everything checks out here. O2 levels at 87 percent. Temperature stable. No 'check engine' lights.

HOUSTON: We copy, Tom.

> *[TOM slowly reaches down and pats JOE on the shoulder. JOE nods and gives a thumbs up sign. TOM responds with the same sign. All of this happens at a painfully slow speed.]*

TOM: Houston, this is Eagle Two. Eagle One seems to have everything under control. I would like to take the opportunity to explore the perimeter and collect further samples.

HOUSTON: Standby, Eagle Two. Will check with Command and Control... OK, you're a go.

TOM: Copy, Houston. Going for a stroll. Shout if you need me, Joe.

JOE: Copy, that, Tom. Watch your step.

TOM: Will do.

> *[TOM turns and heads upstage. He is seen moving around. At first, he collects samples then he motions as if he is playing golf then surfing. Eventually, he makes his way to the stage right side curtain.]*

JOE: Houston, Eagle One. We may have another problem here.

HOUSTON: Go ahead, Eagle One.

JOE: The UHF band is giving me audio reruns of the first episode of Star Trek.

HOUSTON: Please tell me you're joking, Joe.

JOE: (*rambles as he works*) That's me. Joking Joe... You remember the episode where the alien ambassador appears to be a beautiful woman but turns out to be a monster that sucks the salt from your body? ... I think some of the engineers back on earth are the same way... I always thought it was strange that there were never any saltine crackers in the break room but no one would touch my wife's coffee cake... Of course, that could also be attributed to the fact that my wife's coffee cake tastes more like disposed coffee grounds, but she means well.

HOUSTON: Just proves the point that we should limit our salt intake.

JOE: Exactly. Who wants to look like they've just been bear-hugged by a giant octopus... And then there's the whole question of Professor Crater... He called himself the husband of the salt-sucking succubus... I mean, you can see the obvious problems there... Almost got this antenna mount relocated... There it goes... Just need to tighten it down now... Anyway, the professor's sodium-deficient wife is also a shapeshifter who kills by touch... One minute you think you're talking to your mother and then suddenly you are an addition to her spice rack... and the late night romance... that must be tricky... like dancing with a giant squid in heat... and who knows what she thinks about salt shakers!

> [TOM *turns suddenly to face stage right and becomes transfixed.*]

JOE: What do you think, Houston... Houston... Houston, do you copy?

HOUSTON: This is Houston. We, uh, turned the speaker down for a few moments for, uh, maintenance.

JOE: Right.

TOM: Oh... my... God!

HOUSTON: Eagle Two, you are breaking up. Could you repeat your last transmission?

TOM: I, uh, I uh, don't believe it.

JOE: Tom, what is it?

TOM: I saw something in the distance and decided to investigate.

JOE: What did you find?

TOM: A giant black monolith.

JOE: Tom, you're kidding, right?

HOUSTON: Eagle Two, check your levels again, please. You may be experiencing some problems with your suit.

TOM: I'm going to check out this anomaly. This could be an important discovery.

HOUSTON: Uh, Eagle Two, that's a negative. Do not attempt to engage with any unknown substances or structures. I repeat. Do not proceed.

TOM: (*hushed*) I have to. It's practically calling for me to touch it.

JOE: Tom, don't be a fool. You don't know what you have there. Think about what you are doing. Houston!

HOUSTON: Go ahead.

JOE: Permission to retrieve Eagle Two and drag his butt back to the LM.

HOUSTON: You're a go, Eagle One. Move with the greatest haste.

JOE: Copy that. I'm coming buddy!

> [JOE turns to run toward TOM but has to move painfully slow. TOM touches the black curtain on the side of the stage then puts his hand behind the curtain and pulls it back.]

TOM: My hand. My hand! It just went right through that thing... like it wasn't really there... It just kind of tingled for a moment... like there was some kind of static energy in there... like there was... whoa!

> [Both JOE and TOM are pushed by another gust of solar wind. JOE rolls slowly to the ground while TOM is pushed behind the curtain and offstage. JOE works himself back up and notices TOM is gone. He moves toward the spot where TOM was.]

JOE: Tom, Tom! Where are you, Tom? Houston, we have a problem!

HOUSTON: Go ahead.

JOE: Eagle One has been blown right into the object.

HOUSTON: Have you reached the sight yet?

JOE: Almost there... almost there... almost there... Affirmative.

HOUSTON: What do you see?

JOE: (looks stage right behind the curtain) I, uh... I can't believe it. It's Joe, I think... I see him rolling around in there. Now he's changing shape... just like...

HOUSTON: Any chance for an attempt at a rescue, Joe?

JOE: I could maybe reach in there and attempt to pull him out, but...

HOUSTON: What's the problem?

JOE: I just don't want to end up a salt lick.

HOUSTON: This isn't Star Trek, Joe. Pull him out of there.

JOE: Roger, Mission Control.

> *[JOE reaches behind the curtain and takes TOM's hand. He pulls him back onto the stage. TOM cries and whines on the floor like a baby.]*

JOE: Houston, we...

HOUSTON: Yeah, yeah. We have a problem. I know that. Just tell me what it is.

JOE: Tom is acting like a baby.

HOUSTON: Oh come on, Joe. You can be more professional about this. Just because he may not want to come back to the Landing Module with you...

JOE: No. He's really acting like a baby... an actual baby. I mean he's on the ground crying and having a tantrum. Recommendations?

HOUSTON: Well, uh, we, uh... I'll have to get back to you...

JOE: Oh, forget it. I'm pushing him back in.

HOUSTON: Wait, no! You don't know what that thing will do to him.

> *[JOE entices TOM to get up then pushes him back behind the curtain. After a moment he reaches in pulls him back out. This time, TOM stands up but has the demeanor of a teenager.]*

TOM: (to JOE) Dude! That was some kind of wild ride. What am I trippin' on?

HOUSTON: Joe, what's happening? We see you've pulled him out again. What's going on?

JOE: He's turned into a teenager. I think he even has acne.

TOM: Got any chips, man. Hey! What's with this crazy outfit. Not my thing, man. (*reaches to his helmet*) How do you get this thing off?

JOE: (*points behind the curtain*) Wow! She's hot!

TOM: (*turns to see*) Where, man?

> [*JOE pushes TOM behind the curtain again, waits a moment, then pulls him back out again. This time TOM acts like an old man.*]

TOM: (*sounds old*) Hey! What's the matter with you young people today? Do you have to pull me along like I'm some kind of toy wagon? And what's with that outfit? You kids are always coming up with some crazy way to make yourselves up. Creative expression! Hah! Well, I remember when... (*improvise*)

> [*as TOM talks, JOE slowly pushes him back around and pushes him back behind the curtain.*]

HOUSTON: Joe?

JOE: Never mind!

> [*JOE pulls TOM back out again. This time he seems normal at first but speaks with an older woman's voice.*]

JOE: Tom? Is that you? Do you recognize me?

TOM: Of course I recognize you, Joe.

JOE: (*to HOUSTON*) I think I've got him.

HOUSTON: That's a big affirmative. Check his oxygen levels. We think he may be dangerously low.

JOE: Copy.

> [*JOE fiddles with TOM's suit and reads a meter.*]

JOE: Fifteen percent and dropping. He must have used up a lot on his way here.

HOUSTON: OK, Joe. You have to get him back right away. It's going to take time to get him back and he barely has enough oxygen now.

JOE: Understood. (*to TOM*) OK, Tom. We're going to get you back to the LM right away.

TOM: (*with an attitude*) Oh, I know how this goes.

JOE: Um, ok. Good. Now, come on. (*takes TOM's arm and leads him away*)

TOM: This is how it always is, isn't it? I'm in the way. Why don't you move out of the way? You're always in the way. That's what you say. You think I want to control every part of your lives but I don't. I just want to be involved, to be included. Is that so much to ask? I've been through life. I've seen a few things. Maybe you could listen to me once in a while. Maybe you could... (*continues to talk*)

JOE: Can't I just push him back in? Maybe he would be better off in that giant skyscraper.

HOUSTON: What's the problem, Joe?

JOE: I think he's turned into my mother-in-law.

> *[TOM continues to rant and rave as he is guided off stage left by JOE.]*

> *CURTAIN*

Green Grows the Garden

Cast (2M, 1 F)

DETECTIVE SOFIA INNES - A tough but fair police detective who likes to look at the big picture. She wears business clothes and carries a badge.

DETECTIVE PAUL DANIELSEN - A police detective of many years. He is good at what he does but is tired of the job. He wears business clothes and carries a badge.

TOBIAS HASSE "TOBY" - A homeless man. He is dressed in shabby and dirty clothes.

Scene

An interrogation room in a police building. There is a large table in the center of the stage with a chair in the back facing the audience and another chair on the opposite side.

Time

Present.

> [At rise, TOBY is seated in the chair facing the audience. He looks sad, dejected, and nervous. After a few moments, Detectives PAUL and SOFIA enter the room from stage left. PAUL carries some papers in a file folder and throws the file on the table. SOFIA goes to the other side of the table stage right.]

PAUL: (to Toby) Mr. Hasse, you have been arrested for arson. You have been read your rights and you have declined to have a lawyer present here for your questioning. Is that correct?

TOBY: Yes, sir.

SOFIA: You do realize, Mr. Hasse, that a lawyer can be provided for you free of charge?

TOBY: Yes, ma'am.

SOFIA: And yet you still refuse to have one?

TOBY: Don't need one.

PAUL: And why is that?

TOBY: I done it.

PAUL: You done what?

TOBY: I burned it. I lit the fire.

PAUL: Where?

TOBY: In the back where I stay.

SOFIA: You started the fire in the field behind the homeless shelter?

TOBY: Yeah, me. I done it. I burned it. (*looks down*)

SOFIA: Mr. Hasse, do you understand that you have been charged with a very serious crime? You could go to jail.

TOBY: Don't wanna go to jail.

SOFIA: Then you should have a lawyer here helping you.

TOBY: No lawyer. I done it.

PAUL: Would you be willing to put that in writing?

TOBY: Not very good at writin'.

PAUL: We could put you on tape. How about that?

TOBY: Don't care. Just wanna go back.

SOFIA: Back to prison?

TOBY: Back to the shelter.

SOFIA: Prison's where you're going if you say you're guilty and don't have any legal help.

[*TOBY lowers his head and remains silent.*]

PAUL: (*grabs up the papers*) That's good enough for me. Open and shut case. Nice and easy. Let's go. (*heads for the exit stage left*)

SOFIA: Wait, Danielsen. I have a couple more questions.

PAUL: What?

SOFIA: Just hang on a minute. There are some loose ends to tie up.

[*PAUL crosses behind TOBY to stage right and takes SOFIA by the arm.*]

PAUL: (*in a half whisper*) What are you doing? There are no loose ends. He did it. He said so. I believe him. End of story.

SOFIA: Look! I know you have a meeting with Heather or Mandy or whatever her name is but I grew up on the North Shore of Boston and I know what a bad catch smells like.

PAUL: Yes, I have an important meeting with an informant who...

SOFIA: Oh, please. The whole department knows about your 'informant.'

PAUL: (*a beat*) OK. You want to play Joe Friday then go ahead, knock yourself out. But don't take all day.

[*PAUL returns to his place on the stage left side of the table but stands behind TOBY. SOFIA takes the chair facing TOBY and moves it to the stage right side of the table and sits down.*]

SOFIA: (*to TOBY*) Mr. Hasse, uh... (*looks at the file on the table*) Toby. May I call you Toby? (*TOBY is silent*) Toby, tell me about the fire. You say that you started it. How?

TOBY: You already know that.

SOFIA: I want to hear it from you. Tell me how you started the fire.

TOBY: I just took a match and threw it and... boom... it all went up.

SOFIA: Tell me exactly how you started the fire... in detail.

TOBY: (*stares at SOFIA for a moment*) Well, I, uh, put some wood, some loose wood that was lyin' around and piled it all up and then I got some other stuff, you know, leaves and papers and stuff and threw it all on top and then I lit it all.

> [*SOFIA look at TOBY for a moment then glares at PAUL who changes his posture. PAUL moves forward a few steps.*]

PAUL: You were never a Boy Scout where you, Mr. Hasse. (*waits for a response but none comes*) You see, in the Boy Scouts, they teach you how to make a proper fire. The leaves and the papers–what you would call the kindling–is put under the wood. If you put it on top it just burns off and there's no fire.

TOBY: Yeah, well, that's what I did: leaves, paper, wood... fire!

SOFIA: And that's it? That's all you did?

TOBY: Look, lady. What do you want? Why you askin' me all these questions? I piled up some KINDLIN' then I threw some wood down, then I lit a match, and... poof... fire! What more do you need to know?

SOFIA: Well, for starters, you could tell me when you threw the gasoline on the wood.

TOBY: What?

PAUL: (*lets out a deep sigh then sits on the edge of the table*) Gasoline, Toby! The fire was started with gas. You neglected to mention that very important part of the story.

TOBY: Yeah? Well, I just forgot is all.

SOFIA: Toby, you didn't start that fire, did you? Someone else started it. Isn't that so?

TOBY: I started the fire. I burned the garden.

SOFIA: Wait! What did you say? Garden?

> [SOFIA looks at PAUL with a questioning look. PAUL responds with a shrug.]

SOFIA: (to TOBY) Whose garden was it?

> [TOBY looks away.]

SOFIA: Was that your garden, Toby?

TOBY (softly) Yeah.

PAUL: A garden in the middle of a deserted lot?

SOFIA: (slides her chair closer) Toby, tell me about your garden.

TOBY: It was beautiful. There were tomatoes and cucumbers and all kinds of things.

SOFIA: How did it start?

TOBY: Well, it's a funny thing, really. I was walking one day. Not sure where I was. Guess I had a little too much to drink and I got lost. Found myself in a neighborhood I'd never been before. Then I see this garden on the side of one of the houses. It was the most beautiful thing I had ever seen. There were so many colors and things were lined up so perfectly. I just stared at it until someone saw me and sent me away. (a beat) Came back to the shelter and said I wanted to have a garden. I told Mr. Russ and he said he would help me out...

PAUL: Mr. Russ? Who's Mr. Russ?

TOBY: He's my buddy. He works at the shelter.

SOFIA: Mr. Russ got you the seeds so you could start a garden?

TOBY: Yeah. He helped clear a small plot. We even went for walks and stuffed our pockets with good soil to put in the garden. (a beat) It started small. Actually, it didn't start at all. At least, not right away. First couple of years nothing happened. Nothing. I was going to give up but Mr. Russ said it just takes time. Then one day I saw a sprout, and then another and another. Soon I had me a small garden. (*thinks back and smiles*) It was like I had seen that one day: bright colors and straight rows. (*looks at SOPHIA*) You know, it was the one thing I was ever good at and it mostly kept me away from the booze.

SOFIA: So, what happened?

TOBY: My garden kept growing. At first, I ate the vegetables myself. I didn't have to beg for food so much. I kept making the garden bigger and I added more plants. When people saw what I was doing they donated seeds and tools and supplies. Soon I was giving food away not just to my buddies but to anyone who showed up at the shelter.

PAUL: And when did you decide to just burn it all away?

TOBY: Mr. Russ got mad at me. Said I shouldn't have let the garden get so big. Said I was... how did he put it? I was upsetting the apple cart. Kind of funny huh? My garden was upsetting his apples.

SOFIA: Why would your garden make him mad? You were focused on something important. You were even providing food to other people.

TOBY: He said that because of me they wouldn't get any more Christmas presents.

SOFIA: What?

PAUL: (*a beat*) No good deed goes unpunished.

> [*SOFIA looks to PAUL for an explanation but PAUL responds only with a laugh.*]

PAUL: You're not seeing it are you, detective?

SOFIA: Enlighten me.

PAUL: Homeless shelter depends on donations from people who think it needs their money. It relies on a perception of need... (*looks to SOFIA to continue*)

SOFIA: And if that perception changes, so goes the flow of aid... no more Christmas presents.

PAUL: (*to TOBY*) You done good, Mr. Hasse. Too good. You started handing out free food to hungry people from your garden and made your shelter look self-sufficient.

TOBY: That's bad?

PAUL: It is to a shelter that depends on a free flow of donated cash to support itself, its clients, and its staff.

TOBY: Is that why Mr. Russ got mad at me?

PAUL: Yeah. I imagine he got plenty mad.

SOFIA: Toby, did Mr. Russ tell you to start the fire?

TOBY: (*lowers his head*) He was my friend and he got so upset. I didn't know what to do. (*silence*)

SOFIA: Toby... Did he tell you to burn your garden?

> [*TOBY remains silent. Maybe he is heard sobbing.*]

TOBY: You couldn't do it, could you? You couldn't burn down all that work you did, all those plants you loved.

> [*TOBY remains silent and emotional. After a few moments, he shakes his head to indicate a no. After another moment, he speaks.*]

TOBY: He told me to take a long walk. When I came back it was all gone.

SOFIA: Who, Toby? Who told you to take a walk.

TOBY: Mr. Russ.

SOFIA: He told you to take a walk and when you got back your garden was gone?

> [*TOBY hesitates.*]

SOFIA: Toby, if Mr. Russ set fire to your garden... if he killed all those beautiful plants you worked so hard to raise, he's not your friend. (*a beat*) You fed people who were hungry. That was a good thing. It was the right thing no matter what Mr. Russ may have told you. Do the right thing now, Toby. (*a beat*) Did you see Mr. Russ start that fire?

> [TOBY *hesitates again then shakes his head to indicate a yes.*]

PAUL: (*lets out a deep sigh*) Great! There goes my very informative lunch.

SOFIA: (*ignoring PAUL*) Toby, you're free to go, for now.

TOBY: (*lifts his head*) Can I go back to the shelter?

SOFIA: (*pats TOBY's arm*) Sure. And I'm going to see to it that you get a chance to start another garden.

TOBY: Yeah? And can I go see Mr. Russ?

SOFIA: Oh, well. Detective Danielsen and I are going to have a little chat with him but I suspect he may have to go away for a little while.

TOBY: Oh?

SOFIA: There are others, Toby, who want to be your friend, good friends who won't lie to you.

TOBY: (*stares at SOFIA for a moment*) Thank you, ma'am.

PAUL: C'mon. Toby. I'll walk you out and get one of the officers to give you a ride.

> [PAUL *escorts TOBY out. SOFIA sits for a moment where she is, then stands and pushes Toby's chair back under the table. She exits.*]

CURTAIN

The Shootout

Cast (3M)

ZEKE: A cowboy who likes to get into trouble because that's all he knows. He wears a typical cowboy outfit with a gun.

HANK: Another cowboy not unlike Zeke. He has a gun.

MR. TIBBY: The referee for the shootout. He wears more formal clothing and acts like a aristocrat. Maybe he has an English accent. He also has a gun.

Scene

The empty street of a Western town. Perhaps there could be a rotting sign that says: "The Town of Deadrock. ~~Pop. 217~~, ~~Pop. 216~~, ~~Pop. 215~~, Pop. ____."

Time

The late 1800s

> *[At rise, MR. TIBBY is center stage facing the audience. ZEKE and HANK are in front of him facing away from each other. They each have their hands close to their pistols in their holsters.]*

MR. TIBBY: Alright, gentleman. You will each take five steps then turn and shoot.

ZEKE: Five steps?

HANK: I thought it was supposed to be ten steps.

MR. TIBBY: It's five steps.

ZEKE: Why ain't it ten steps?

MR. TIBBY: An inconvenience caused by increasing amounts of traffic, I'm afraid.

HANK: Traffic?

ZEKE: What's he talking about?

MR. TIBBY: With the advent of the railway in the county there has been more traffic through town and more visitors resulting in further parking challenges such that the town has had to divide the main thoroughfare into two narrow one-way streets.

HANK: What did he say?

ZEKE: Can't take ten steps.

MR. TIBBY: That is correct. Now if we can proceed. At the count of five, each of you will…

ZEKE: Yeah, we got that.

HANK: Just get to the countin'.

> [*Each time MR. TIBBY counts off, both ZEKE and HANK take a large step forward.*]

MR. TIBBY: OK, gentlemen. Here we go. One…

HANK: Wait!

MR. TIBBY: What is it?

HANK: (*turns around*) How do I know he won't cheat? He could turn around at three or four and shoot me full of holes before I have a chance.

ZEKE: (*turns and steps toward HANK*) I don't need to cheat to beat you, you good-for-nothin'…

HANK: (*steps up into ZEKE's face*) You cheat at cards, you cheat with women, you'd cheat your own mother.

ZEKE: Shut up you. You ain't never seen my mother play cards. She's vicious. Makes me bet my own allowance.

MR. TIBBY: (*pulls the two apart and holds his own gun up*) There won't be any cheating here. For starters, each of you only has one bullet and I've got a full gun. We got rules and cheaters die. *(a beat)* Now, turn around and we will begin again.

> *[ZEKE and HANK turn around and hold their guns up.]*

MR. TIBBY: One… Two…

ZEKE: Hang on a second.

MR. TIBBY: Now what?

ZEKE: *(walks back)* Who exactly are you?

MR. TIBBY: I am the adjudicator for this gunfight.

HANK: *(walks back)* The Judy what?

ZEKE: Why can't we just shoot each other like we used to do?

MR. TIBBY: Because this town voted to enforce rules and regulations on shootouts. The good people decided that they had had enough of wanton violence and reckless mayhem. They established proper procedures, one of which requires you to retain my services.

ZEKE: Uh-huh.

HANK: What did he say?

ZEKE: Sumpin about regulations.

MR. TIBBY: Could we get on with it, gentleman? I have another appointment in an hour.

ZEKE and HANK: Oh, yeah, sure, sure. *(they turn around)*

MR. TIBBY: One… Two… Three…

HANK: *(walks back)* I just have one question.

MR. TIBBY: Oh, for the love of Shakespeare! What is it?

HANK: It's just… well, I don't quite remember what this fight is all about. By the time we signed the contract and reserved the street and all, I done forgot what it was all for.

ZEKE: (*walks back and looks at HANK*) Because you, you pesky dog, called my daddy an angry coot.

MR. TIBBY: Oh my!

HANK: I didn't call your pop an angry coot. I called your brother an angry coot. He's a hothead and you know it.

ZEKE: Yeah, I know it. He's been tossed in the slammer more times than I can count cause he can't keep himself down. I've even put him in there a few times myself.

HANK: So, what's the problem?

ZEKE: The problem is you ALSO called my mammy a penny pinchin' old lady.

HANK: That's because your mother came into my sister's dress shop demanding that everything be on sale. She says everything is over-priced. My sister runs a good business.

ZEKE: Well, maybe everything IS overpriced. Maybe she's into gougin' people for money or something.

MR. TIBBY: Actually, I have found her prices to be quite fair. They certainly are comparable to other shops in the area.

[*HANK and ZEKE turn and stare at MR. TIBBY.*]

HANK: How many times you been IN my sister's store?

MR. TIBBY: Oh about... (*change of tone*) Never mind! Let's not forget that you two hate each other. Now, work that anger boys! Feel it!

[*HANK and ZEKE look back at each other.*]

MR. TIBBY: You boys have been destroying each other and your families for years. We can't have that anymore. This town deserves some peace. Now, turn around and let's do this properly.

[*HANK and ZEKE turn around.*]

MR. TIBBY: Here we go. One... Two... Three... Four...

ZEKE: Why?

MR. TIBBY: What?

ZEKE: (*turns around*) Why?

MR. TIBBY: Why what?

ZEKE: (*walks back*) Why we been fightin'?

HANK: (*walks back*) Just cause! Do you really need a reason? You and I fight. Our families feud. That's just the way it is.

ZEKE: Yeah, but don't you ever wonder why? I mean, if I'm going to go and kill you I ought to at least know the what for!

HANK: You mean you want to know why you're going to be shot?

ZEKE: So you say! Either way, I want to know why.

HANK: Well, if HE wants to know why, then so do I. (*to Mr. TIBBY*) So, why?

MR. TIBBY: Your two families have been fighting for decades.

ZEKE: You ain't said why.

MR. TIBBY: Water rights. There is a creek that runs right between the plots of both your families. Each one claims the right to use the water for their livestock and crops and both have sought to deny those rights to the other.

HANK: We've been feudin' over water?

MR. TIBBY: That's right.

ZEKE: Seems kind of silly.

MR. TIBBY: Silly? Oh no! Water is serious business out here in the old West. Water is life. The family who controls the water controls the land... and the money.

ZEKE: Still seems kind of silly.

HANK: And a waste of time.

ZEKE: Waste of time?

HANK: Well, yeah. There's no need to be feudin' over that.

ZEKE: Are you sayin' we ain't good enough to have that water?

HANK: Well, you ain't. But, that's not what I'm talking about.

ZEKE: What are you talkin' about, then?

HANK: I'm talking about setting up a trust for the land.

ZEKE: Well, I don't trust no land of yours.

HANK: (*without a change of tone*) No, a community land trust: a piece of property acquired and held in trust in perpetuity by a non-profit entity on behalf of the community with the ability to enter into an equitable leasing arrangement.

ZEKE: (*after a few moments of silence*) Oh, that!

HANK: In other words, both our families could use the water from the creek as long as we don't damage the property.

ZEKE: Oh, well... That sounds like a good idea to me. (*to MR. TIBBY*) Ain't that a good idea?

MR. TIBBY: What? No! That's a terrible idea. It's a downright ghastly idea. You two can't be standing here solving your problems. You signed a contract! People are expecting a gunfight and if you don't give them one then I don't get paid, the undertaker gets no business, people lose their bets, and there will be no after-shooting party... all kinds of terrible things will happen.

HANK: We signed a contract?

MR. TIBBY: Well your families signed one on your behalf.

ZEKE: How considerate of them.

MR. TIBBY: And for good reason.

HANK: How's that?

MR. TIBBY: Because your families know how to keep a good feud going. Think about it. All you have ever known all your life is that you have been fighting. The feud's the thing! To fight or not to fight is NOT the question. The feud is what you live and die for. It is your reason for being and it's what makes you feel most alive.

ZEKE: Until you ain't!

MR. TIBBY: But that's the excitement of it all. You live your life on the edge of death. You fight to survive and to protect your family–flawed as they may be. You can't just give that up. You need this feud–both of you. It's who you are!

[HANK and ZEKE look at each other and shrug.]

HANK: OK, then. I guess that's it.

ZEKE: Yup. That decides it.

HANK: There is only one thing left to do.

ZEKE: Yup. We gotta do what we were meant to do.

MR. TIBBY: That's the spirit boys! No use denying destiny. Now spin right around... that's it... and let's get this done. Here we go. One... Two... Three... Four... (a beat) Five!

[HANK and ZEKE turn around, point their guns at MR. TIBBY, and shoot. MR. TIBBY dies a long and dramatic Shakespearean death.]

HANK: (watching) How long is this going to take?

ZEKE: Don't know. They should have given us more than one bullet.

MR. TIBBY: (after his long scene) OK. I'm dead now.

HANK: Finally!

ZEKE: So, tell me more about this land thingee.

HANK: The community land trust?

ZEKE: Yeah. How's that work?

HANK: Well...

[HANK and ZEKE exit together as they discuss their plans.] <u>CURTAIN</u>

Dinner at Dinah's

<u>Cast (2W, 1 M)</u>

NELL: A bombastic middle-aged woman who hides her insecurities behind her lavish clothes and personality.

DINAH: A middle-aged woman with a less robust but still effusive personality.

STAGEHAND: A typical theater stagehand.

Note: All roles can be of any ethnicity.

<u>Scene</u>

The stage should be left in whatever state it was in at the end of the previous ten-minute play.

Note: NELL and DINAH need to be seated in the audience before the play begins.

<u>Time</u>

Present.

> *[At rise (or not), the stage is empty. After several moments, the house lights go up and the STAGEHAND walks on stage to address the audience.]*

STAGEHAND: Ladies and gentlemen, I'm sorry to have to tell you that we are having some technical difficulty with the next play. We are working as hard as we can to resolve the issue and will begin as soon as we can. In the meantime, we ask for your patience and understanding. Thank you very much. (*starts to exit*)

NELL: (*from audience*) How long?

STAGEHAND: (*turns back*) I beg your pardon?

NELL: How long will we have to wait?

STAGEHAND: It won't be long. It's just a little technical glitch. Thank you all for your...

NELL: Is that what you call it now? A technical glitch?

STAGEHAND: Well, that's what it is.

NELL: I know how you theater people are. You do your little plays and cry your eyes out then you go and hit the bars afterward and forget that you have to do it all over again the next day and then the next day comes and... well... 'technical glitch'!

STAGEHAND: Ma'am, I assure you that it's nothing like that. There's a...

NELL: (*stands up*) You see all these people here? If you don't put something up on that stage in the next sixty seconds, all those phones resting quietly in their pockets or bags are going to come out and people will tweet and post and snap and gram and then they won't care anymore about your technical glitch. They'll be transfixed by dancing cats and bad meals with even worse names.

DINAH: (*stands*) Nell?

STAGEHAND: (*to NELL*) Ma'am, please take your seat.

NELL: Do you have any idea how many different ways people have come up with to name their meatloaf?

STAGEHAND: I'm sure...

DINAH: Nell, is that you?

STAGEHAND: (*notices Dinah*) Please, please! Everyone take your seats.

DINAH: Nellie Marston, is that really you?

NELL: (*turns to see DINAH*) Dinah? Oh my goodness, Dinah! How long has it been?

DINAH: I don't know. I...

NELL: Well, don't just stand there, girl. Bring it in.

> [NELL and DINAH both make a big deal of working their way from their seats to a space in the aisle between them. They hug. DINAH looks a little uncertain about the meeting. STAGEHAND exits.]

NELL: So, how are you?

DINAH: Oh... good, good. You?

NELL: Oh, just great. What have you been up to?

DINAH: Well I, uh... I just got married.

NELL: (*with mixed emotions*) Married. You're married! Well, that's just, uh, wonderful. Married! Imagine that. You're married. Is he, uh, wonderful?

DINAH: Wonderful? Oh yes. He's warm and kind and... wonderful!

NELL: Oh yes. Well, that's just, uh... wonderful.

> [NELL and DINAH share an awkward moment.]

NELL: (*looking around*) So, where is Mr. Wonderful?

DINAH: Oh, he had to work tonight.

NELL: Not much of a play-goer, huh?

DINAH: No Tom doesn't...

NELL: Tom?

DINAH: Yeah, his name is Tom.

NELL: Isn't it a small world? My last boyfriend's name was Tom.

DINAH: (*looks embarrassed*) Oh... really? What a small world.

NELL: Yeah.

DINAH: (*trying to recover*) Yeah. (*pause*) So, tell me. What about you?

NELL: What about me?

DINAH: Married yet?

NELL: Married? Oh my! Married? (*laughs*) But of course I'm married. I'm locked in a veritable state of matrimonial bliss with the man of my dreams.

DINAH: How wonderful. Is he here with you?

NELL: (*stalling*) Well, um... yes. Of course.

> *[NELL finds a random man in the audience and gets near him.]*

NELL: Here he is, the lucky guy!

DINAH: Well, introduce us. What's his name?

NELL: His name? Of course! Tell her your name, sweetheart.

> *[NELL encourages the man to tell his name.]*

NELL: His name is {*name*}. Meet the man of my dreams... {*name*}.

DINAH: Why is he sitting all the way over here?

NELL: Oh, well, we got our tickets at the last minute. It was all they had left. But it's OK isn't it honey? We don't have to sit next to each other to share a great time together.

DINAH: Oh, that's so romantic. What does he do for work?

NELL: Oh, well. He's, uh... a professional weightlifter. I mean, look at these highly toned and pumped muscles. He's a well crafted and honed machine. And smart too! He's got at least two Ph.D.s in quantum biological stamp collecting or some such thing and well, he's just soooo cute!

DINAH: Oh! I'm so happy for you, Nell. I suppose you've completely forgotten about Tom, uh... right?

NELL: Oh, yes. Completely out of my mind. Tom who? (*they laugh*)

DINAH: Oh, well. It was so good to see you.

NELL: And you too. (*they hug*) I suppose we should take our seats.

> [*NELL and DINAH crawl over people to get back to their seats. As they do, the STAGEHAND returns to the stage and tries to ignore them.*]

STAGEHAND: Ladies and gentlemen, on behalf of the theater I must really apologize for the delay but we will have the problem resolved right away and then we can begin our next play very soon. In the meantime...

NELL: Black coffee.

STAGEHAND: What?

NELL: Lots of black coffee should do the trick. In the meantime (*mocking him*)... what are you going to do for us?

STAGEHAND: Me?

NELL: You look strong, healthy, and... sober. Why don't you do a little song and dance for us while we wait? A little soft shoe? Maybe some gymnastics. I bet you used to do some mean flips, huh?

STAGEHAND: Well, I...

NELL: Go ahead. Tell us all about it.

STAGEHAND: (*proudly*) I must admit that I...

DINAH: (*stands*) Nell?

NELL: (*ignores the STAGEHAND and stands*) Dinah? What is it?

DINAH: I'm really sorry about you and Tom.

NELL: Dinah, I'm sorry too. In fact, I have to tell you something. I lied to you.

> [*The STAGEHAND gets frustrated at being shouted over and exits.*]

DINAH: About being married?

NELL: Yeah, how did you know?

DINAH: I had my suspicions.

NELL: Can we talk?

DINAH: Sure, Nell. Bring it in.

> [NELL and DINAH make their way through the audience back to where they gathered in the aisle. They hug.]

NELL: Oh, I'm so sorry to have lied to you before. It's just that I went through a terrible break up with my last boyfriend, Tom.

DINAH: Yes. It must have been awful after all that time.

NELL: Yes, yes it was. It seemed like it was going so well. I mean we did practically everything together and then it was suddenly all over.

DINAH: I know.

NELL: What?

DINAH: I mean I know how hard that must have been.

NELL: It was. But the past is past right? We have to learn to move on. One door closes and another opens, isn't that so?

DINAH: Uh-huh.

NELL: Enough about me. What about you? What's your man like?

DINAH: (suddenly uncomfortable) Well, uh… he's… You know, just an average guy.

NELL: Is he tall like Tom was?

DINAH: Well, yeah.

NELL: Is he a hockey fan like Tom was?

DINAH: As a matter of fact, he is.

NELL: Does he play golf even in the rain?

DINAH: Like you said, small world.

NELL: (*starts to laugh*) Oh my goodness, you're right. What a small world it is. Maybe they just pump these guys out of a factory or something. Next, you'll tell me he has horn-rimmed glasses and a mole on his left shoulder.

> [*NELL keeps laughing until she notices DINAH is not responding or laughing.*]

NELL: Dinah, it was a joke. Get it? Not every man is going to have horn-rimmed glasses and a mole on his left shoulder like Tom did... unless... (*comes to a realization*). You didn't!

DINAH: Didn't what?

NELL: Steal my Tom from right under my nose.

DINAH: I didn't steal him. He came to me. He joined my bowling league and we happened to have adjoining lanes and we just started talking, that's all. One thing led to another...

NELL: Which led to you taking away the love of my life.

DINAH: I didn't want to hurt you. It just happened this way. You have to believe me!

NELL: But why? Why would he do this to me? We were so close. I never left his side.

DINAH: But that's just it, Nell. He said you were suffocating him. He felt like he couldn't breathe. He didn't know what to do so he just ran away.

NELL: Oh, Dinah! How could he say such a thing? How could he possibly say that I was suffocating him? You know how shy and reserved I am.

DINAH: Well, uh...

NELL: (*hugs DINAH*) Oh, Dinah. It's me, me! I chased him away. I don't deserve him. He deserves someone wonderful like you. Someone... special...just...like... you!

> [*In the last sentence, NELL squeezes DINAH harder*]

with each word.]

DINAH: Nnnnnell!

NELL: (*seeing what she's done*) Oh, Dinah, I'm so sorry.

DINAH: (*catching her breath*) No, no. It's alright. I can see you're very upset.

NELL: Listen, I'm just going to go back to my seat and watch the next play.

DINAH: Oh, OK. Will you be alright?

NELL: Sure, sure. I'll be fine. I'll see you after the show.

DINAH: Yeah, later.

> *[NELL and DINAH make their way through the audience and settle back into their seats for a few awkward moments.]*

DINAH: (*stands*) Nell! Hey, Nell!

NELL: (*stands*) Dinah?

DINAH: Nell, listen! I just had a fantastic idea. Why don't you come over for dinner Saturday night?

NELL: Dinner? With you and Tom? Oh no, I couldn't. (*starts to sit*)

DINAH: No, listen! It would be your chance to show him you're over him, that you have moved on, that you're a new person. Besides, I want us all to be friends.

NELL: (*stands again*) Oh, I don't know, Dinah.

DINAH: It'll be fun, like old times. (*pause*) We'll find you a date.

NELL: A date?

DINAH: Sure. Someone fun and interesting.

NELL: Where am I going to find someone like that?

> *[The STAGEHAND enters]*

STAGEHAND: Ladies and gentlemen, I am very pleased to tell

you...

NELL: Your sign! You're very pleased to tell us your sign.

STAGEHAND: My sign?

NELL: Yeah, what sign are you?

STAGEHAND: I'm a Libra.

NELL: Libra! Hear that Nell, he's a Libra. (*to STAGEHAND*) Ever had a felony conviction?

STAGEHAND: What kind of question is that?

NELL: Are you stalling in front of all these people? Maybe it's because...

STAGEHAND: No! I have never had a felony conviction.

NELL: Member of an extremist political group?

STAGEHAND: No! What is this?

NELL: Serial killer? Member of a pseudo-religious cult? Drug dealer? Cosmetic surgery? Keep a pet python?

STAGEHAND: Uh... no!

NELL: Free on Saturday night?

STAGEHAND: No!

NELL: You're a terrible liar but you have a good heart. I'll see you after the show, handsome. (*to Dinah*) He'll do. (*sits*)

DINAH: Saturday night, then! (*sits*)

NELL: Saturday night!

STAGEHAND: (*trying to recover*) Uh, ladies and gentleman, the next play is ready to begin. (*exits*)

CURTAIN

Find the Mole

Note: The characters can be played by any gender or ethnicity.

AGENT DOOR - A spy for some unnamed agency. Wears business clothes and a long coat.

AGENT WINDOW - Also a spy for the same unknown agency and similarly dressed but less competent. He speaks with a fake English accent.

Scene

A secret rendezvous point. It can simply be two chairs turned sideways and facing away from each other.

Time

The present.

> *[At rise, AGENT DOOR is sitting in one of the chairs reading a paper. After a few moments, AGENT WINDOW enters and sits in the other chair. AGENT WINDOW opens up a comic book.]*

AGENT WINDOW: It's a nice day to fly. (*no response*) I say, it's a nice day to fly.

AGENT DOOR: A kite.

AGENT WINDOW: Yes, I'm alright. How are you?

AGENT DOOR: No, a kite. You're supposed to say it's a nice day to fly a kite.

AGENT WINDOW: Well, it certainly is. The sun is out, the birds are singing.

AGENT DOOR: No, you fool. It's your callsign. Now try it again.

AGENT WINDOW: Oh right, the callsign. (*collects himself*) It's a nice day to... fly a kite.

AGENT DOOR: (*without emotion*) It's a shame I don't have one.

AGENT WINDOW (*turns around*) Oh that really is a shame. I passed a shop on my way here. I bet we could get one for you...

AGENT DOOR: Turn around and be quiet before someone notices we are talking.

AGENT WINDOW: (*turns around and opens his comic book*) Oh, right. We don't want anyone to notice there are two people talking on a public bench. You're Agent Door?

AGENT DOOR: Quiet! No names! (*a beat*) You have been called to this meeting because we have learned some rather disturbing news.

AGENT WINDOW: And what would that be?

AGENT DOOR: The Intelligence Division has determined that there may be a mole in the department.

AGENT WINDOW: A mole? Oh, that's terrible. Those little critters can dig tunnels for miles and they're smelly, too.

AGENT DOOR: No, not that kind of mole. An informant, a turn-coat.

AGENT WINDOW: There's an informant in the department?

AGENT DOOR: Yes! We have to be very careful. It could be anyone, anywhere. We can trust no one.

AGENT WINDOW: No one?

AGENT DOOR: No one.

AGENT WINDOW: (*pulls out his gun with one hand and points it at AGENT DOOR*) Then hold it right there, buster.

AGENT DOOR: What are you doing?

AGENT WINDOW: I am apprehending the mollusk.

AGENT DOOR: It's mole and I am not it.

AGENT WINDOW: (*touches his nose*) Not it either.

AGENT DOOR: (*sighs*) Listen! The chief called this meeting because he thought we could be trusted to work together. The informant is in deep hiding which means it is neither one of us so put your gun away and sit down before someone takes notice.

AGENT WINDOW: Alright. What do you want me to do?

AGENT DOOR: I need some information.

AGENT WINDOW: OK.

AGENT DOOR: First off, why are you talking with that ridiculous accent? You're not British.

AGENT WINDOW: It makes me sound clandestine and mysterious. You know, like James Bond.

AGENT DOOR: Why you think that's a good idea is a mystery to me.

AGENT WINDOW: (*with accents, if possible*) Would you prefer an Indian accent? Maybe I should be French or Arabic. Maybe I could be a double agent from Mother Russia.

AGENT DOOR: Maybe you could be quiet and listen to me.

AGENT WINDOW: (*in a Jamaican accent*) Yeah, mon. I could do dat.

AGENT DOOR: You maintain some contacts within the department?

AGENT WINDOW: (*back to the first accent*) I do.

AGENT DOOR: (*reaches into his pocket and pulls out a folded piece of paper*) I have here a list of four names.

    [AGENT DOOR gives the paper to AGENT WINDOW

who starts to unfold it.]

AGENT DOOR: No, don't read it now. Put it away. (*a beat*) We believe that the mole may be one of those four people. For now, I will refer to them as Peter, Paul, Mary, and Larry.

AGENT WINDOW: Peter, Paul, Mary, and Larry?

AGENT DOOR: Right. Now, I'm going to give you a message to pass on to each of them.

AGENT WINDOW: Easy enough.

AGENT DOOR: The message is: The President will have a cheeseburger...

AGENT WINDOW: The president eats cheeseburgers?

AGENT DOOR: Well, why WOULDN'T he eat cheeseburgers? That's not important. The message...

AGENT WINDOW: It's just that he has his own cooks and can eat anything he wants. Why would he want some plain old cheeseburger? I mean, what kind of example does that set for the kids of this country? He should be on TV saying 'hey kids, look at me eating my spinach and carrot sandwich.'

AGENT DOOR: That's not the point! The important thing to remember is that each person on your list will be given a different day in the message. For Peter, the message will be: The President will have a cheeseburger on Monday. For Paul, the message will be: The President will have a cheeseburger on Tuesday. For Mary it will be on Wednesday and Larry will have Thursday.

AGENT WINDOW: Peter's on Monday, Paul has Tuesday, Larry gets Wednesday and Mary is Thursday.

AGENT DOOR: No. It's Mary before Larry.

AGENT WINDOW: Mary before Larry, Wednesday before Thursday. What happens on Friday?

AGENT DOOR: Mary's getting married. That's why we have to do this next week. After the wedding, we will lose our opportunity to catch the traitor. They are all going to the Canary Islands.

AGENT WINDOW: Who will marry Mary?

AGENT DOOR: Larry.

AGENT WINDOW: Mary marries Larry then they ferry to the Canaries?

AGENT DOOR: Uh, right. The plan is that one of them will pass off the information to our enemy. When we intercept the message, the day of the week that is mentioned will tip us off to exactly who is the mole.

AGENT WINDOW: Oh, I get it. If the Contact says the President will have a cheeseburger on Monday then Paul is the informant.

AGENT DOOR: No, Peter.

AGENT WINDOW: Peter? Not Paul? Did Peter steal the cheeseburger?

AGENT DOOR: Peter did not steal any cheeseburgers.

AGENT WINDOW: Maybe Larry stole it. He must have owed Paul money.

AGENT DOOR: What?

AGENT WINDOW: He had to rob Peter to pay Paul.

AGENT DOOR: No, no, no. Peter is Monday. Paul is Tuesday.

AGENT WINDOW: Oh, right. Peter, Paul, Mary, and Larry.

AGENT DOOR: Now you've got it. All you have to do is deliver those messages in the correct order to the contacts on your list.

AGENT WINDOW: Right. No Problem. I've got it.

> [AGENT WINDOW *pats the piece of paper in his coat several times. At first, he taps it quickly and confidently but eventually slows down the tapping.*]

AGENT WINDOW: Wait just a minute!

AGENT DOOR: What is it, Agent Window? You should be on your way to fulfilling your mission.

AGENT WINDOW: The key to being a great investigator is in paying attention to the details.

AGENT DOOR: Yeah, so?

AGENT WINDOW: (*rises slowly*) Just exactly how did you know about my contacts anyway? They are called 'secret informants' for a reason. It is because they are meant to be secret and because they are meant to inform me of things... like who might be a mule.

AGENT DOOR: Mole!

AGENT WINDOW: Mole, right! And how is it that you know so much about this subterranean creature?

AGENT DOOR: For the last time, it's not an animal, it's a person giving away important secrets.

AGENT WINDOW: And how do you know it's not an animal? It could be anyONE or anyTHING as far as you know. How do you know someone's cute little Pomeranian is not secretly recording our conversation right now or one of those hummingbirds isn't snapping pictures?

AGENT DOOR: Just listen to yourself! The only way that could happen is if some PERSON was in charge.

AGENT WINDOW: That's right. Someone has to be in charge. Someone has to be in control, someone who knows things like... the names of my contacts. No one could have known them. That could only mean one thing. (*pulls out his gun with one hand and points it at AGENT DOOR*) YOU are the moron!

AGENT DOOR: (*shouting*) Mole!

AGENT WINDOW: Yes, yes, yes. Mole! Whatever little furry thing it is... you are it! Now stand up and put your hands behind your back. You are under arrest.

[*AGENT DOOR rises slowly from his seat. He looks*

angry as he puts his hands behind him and comes closer to AGENT WINDOW.]

AGENT WINDOW: You have the right to be guilty. Anything I say will probably be used against you. You have the right to an intern while I call my lawyer. (*hand starts shaking*)

AGENT DOOR: You're doing it wrong!

AGENT WINDOW: What?

AGENT DOOR: That is not the proper way to hold your gun against a perp. (*pause*) Hold the weapon with both hands. You're right-handed so the right hand has forward pressure while the left-hand resists the right. Right foot behind the left with weight mostly on the left and the gun at eye level.

[AGENT WINDOW follows AGENT DOOR's instructions. When done, AGENT DOOR walks up to the tip of the gun and places it against his head or chest.]

AGENT DOOR: Now, shoot me!

AGENT WINDOW: What?

AGENT DOOR: Shoot me! You claim that I am a traitor to my country and have divulged information that has compromised our agents. It is your duty to shoot me.

AGENT WINDOW: (*panicking*) Only if you resist arrest or threaten my safety or the safety of others.

[AGENT DOOR pulls out his gun and points it at AGENT WINDOW]

AGENT DOOR: You mean like this? (*a beat*) Now shoot me, Agent Window!

AGENT WINDOW: I... I... I... can't! (*lowers his gun*)

AGENT DOOR: The reason I know the name of your contacts is because I am the one who assigned them to you. (*puts his gun away*)

AGENT WINDOW Oh! (*sits down dejected*)

AGENT DOOR: You very nearly killed a falsely accused fellow agent.

AGENT WINDOW: (*breaks down*) Oh, I'm a terrible agent. I can't seem to do anything right.

AGENT DOOR: No argument here. (*paces back and forth for a moment*) You know, all this time we have been looking for a mole–someone in the organization who was clever enough to steal information and give it to our enemies who then used that information against us. I now believe that we may have gotten it wrong all along.

AGENT WINDOW: What are you talking about?

AGENT DOOR: I think maybe you were right.

AGENT WINDOW: I was?

AGENT DOOR: We don't have a mole. We have a moron and that moron is you. No one has been stealing information that threatened our operations. It's just been you screwing them up and, in the process, endangering our agents. (*a beat*) Tell me something Agent Window. How did you ever make it out of the Academy?

AGENT WINDOW: My father.

AGENT WINDOW: Ah, yes. The senator.

AGENT WINDOW: Every low test score, every failed qualification, every poor evaluation was remedied by his power and his money.

AGENT DOOR: But it's the rest of us who are paying for it!

AGENT WINDOW: Oh, what am I going to do? All I ever wanted to do is be an agent. (*a beat*) Are you going to send me up?

> [AGENT DOOR does not respond right away but continues to pace. After some thought, he responds.]

AGENT DOOR: No. I think there may still be a good use for your talents.

AGENT WINDOW: I have talents?

AGENT DOOR: (*ignores him*) I have another assignment for you.

AGENT WINDOW: Really?

> [*AGENT DOOR grabs the paper from his seat and gives it to AGENT WINDOW.*]

AGENT DOOR: Sometimes there are coded messages buried right in front of our own eyes. This section here, for example. (*points*)

AGENT WINDOW: The Want Ads?

AGENT DOOR: Yes. They can be full of encrypted messages. I want you to go through them carefully–one by one–until you find one that looks suspicious. Then, I want you to apply for the position advertised and go deep undercover.

AGENT WINDOW: (*hopeful*) Yeah?

AGENT DOOR: You will remain undercover for quite some time. I want you to make a careful and detailed file of their activities then you will report back to me in say... six months, or maybe a year or so if things go well.

AGENT WINDOW: I got it, sir. You can count on me. I will undertake this assignment with the greatest of enthusiasm.

AGENT DOOR: Good to know. I will contact you when I am ready. Do not make any attempts to contact me.

AGENT WINDOW: Understood.

AGENT DOOR: (*takes AGENT WINDOW's hand*) Good luck, agent.

AGENT WINDOW: Thank you, sir.

AGENT DOOR: (*starts to exit then stops*) Oh, and tell your father I said hello. (*exits*)

<u>CURTAIN</u>

We Three

Cast (1F, 1M, 1A)

PAST - A soft-spoken and gentle female dressed all in white.

PRESENT - A flamboyant and mostly jolly male. He wears bright clothes that contain a lot of dark green.

FUTURE - A mostly silent person dressed in a dark hoodie who always keeps the hood over his or her face.

Scene

A table at a local bar and pub. There are typical bar sounds in the background and the lights are low. On the table are drinks, some snacks, and some personal belongings.

Time

The present.

> [At rise, the three are sitting at a table. PAST sits on the left, PRESENT sits on the right, and FUTURE sits in between them. They are each nursing a drink and there are some snacks on the table. For several moments the three just sit and watch people in the pub.]

PRESENT: Well now. Isn't this festive?

PAST: Hmph!

PRESENT: (*to PAST*) Not having a good time?

PAST: (*shrugs her shoulders, then unconvincingly*) Sure.

> [PRESENT gives PAST a look then turns his attention

to FUTURE.]

PRESENT: (*to FUTURE*) How about you? Having a good time?

> *[FUTURE simply turns his/her head to PRESENT then turns back to watching the party in a very slow and emotionless manner.]*

PAST: That's the most excited I've ever seen him/her.

PRESENT: That makes you the odd one out. What's up with you anyway?

PAST: Look at those people. Look at them all. I mean, just look!

PRESENT: Well, it is a holiday party, after all.

PAST: So, what? People can stroll into somebody's house full of lights and baubles and fattening foods and just forget about all their troubles?

PRESENT: That's the idea.

PAST: They're all just so happy!

PRESENT: And why does that upset you so? Isn't that what we want–people full of goodwill and cheer?

PAST: Yeah, well, I guess so. But it does sort of put us out of a job, doesn't it?

PRESENT: If the whole world was at this party I suppose it would but there's still a lot of misery. There will always be someone out there who needs our help.

PAST: Maybe so, but why us? Why do we have to save everyone? Maybe we've done enough.

PRESENT: First, you were complaining because everyone's having a good time. Now you're saying we've done enough. What's going on?

PAST: Oh, I don't know. I think maybe we've done all we can. It's time for something else. They don't need us anymore.

PRESENT: How can you even say such a thing? There's no shortage of hatred and intolerance out there. They need us now more than ever.

PAST: That's just it. No matter how hard we work, no matter how many we try to reach, there's always more pain and suffering. (*a beat*) I just don't know anymore. It's like trying to stop a tsunami with a paper cup. (*sighs*) I'm just tired, is all.

PRESENT: You can't look at it that way. If you look at everything at once, you get overwhelmed. It becomes too much. But if you look at a small part, it doesn't look so bad. We help one person and then that person helps others and, slowly, you make a small dent on the wreckage of humanity.

PAST: You're just fooling yourself into thinking you're doing something when, in reality, you do nothing more than just make yourself feel good.

PRESENT: Well, that's a start, isn't it? If, as you say, I am doing nothing more than making myself feel good at least I am moving in a positive direction and refuse to fall into the dump heap of misery that others so enjoy wallowing in.

PAST: You? Ha! You wouldn't know how to be miserable if you tried.

PRESENT: And why should I? Instead of being mired in the past like you, I prefer to live in the moment. I refuse to let memories weigh me down (*looks at FUTURE*) or to let fears of what might happen paralyze me. We have to keep trying.

FUTURE: (*in an ominous and drawn-out voice*) Why?

PRESENT: Why? You ask me why? You? You know better than most what might be if no one cared. Surely you have seen the possibilities.

FUTURE: (*same ominous voice*) I have.

PRESENT: You know better than anyone what would happen if we just gave up. They can choose to make a difference and we can show them how.

PAST: Yet they rarely do anyway.

PRESENT: It's because they don't see the truth that surrounds them.

PAST: (*to FUTURE*) Ugh! Here he goes again!

PRESENT: They believe they are separate beings and they spend their lives fortifying that separation with money, status, titles, belongings, and any number of other trappings they think are important.

PAST: (*rolling her hands as if to move things along*) But what they don't realize is...

PRESENT: What they don't realize is that the sense of separation they work so hard to maintain is false. Few of the things they think are important are really of any value at all because...

PAST: (*mocking*) Because everything is actually connected, blah, blah, blah, and what's really important is nurturing that interdependence, or spider web, or cosmic fishing net, or whatever metaphor you're into these days.

PRESENT: Wow! I had no idea you were this disillusioned. (*to FUTURE*) You feel this way too?

> [*FUTURE nods his/her head in large slow movements. PRESENT lets out a sigh and plays with his drink.*]

PRESENT: (*after a time*) Hey! You two remember this one guy we visited a while back? It was in London, I think. He had to be one of the crankiest old geezers we had ever come across.

PAST: The penny-pinching rich banker with the ratty clothes?

PRESENT: That's the one.

PAST: Who could forget that grumpy old grouch?

PRESENT: I don't think he cared about anyone or anything but his own money.

PAST: It was Christmas Eve, wasn't it?

PRESENT: Not that the day meant anything to him. He was a piece of work, huh?

PAST: I had my doubts at first but, by the time we were done with him, he was dancing in the street in his pajamas and throwing his money at anyone he met.

PRESENT: One of our finest moments.

PAST: (*laughs*) Yeah.

PRESENT: The number of poor and destitute in that part of town declined sharply that day.

PAST: So all we have to do to save the world is change the dreams of rich people?

PRESENT: Of course not! Money isn't the only way to affect change. Have you forgotten the others we have helped?

PAST: I don't forget. I just sometimes choose not to remember.

PRESENT: (*thinks for a moment*) How about the guy from India? He certainly wasn't rich.

PAST: The skinny guy? The one who rarely ate any food and his clothes barely hung on to his body? What about him?

PRESENT: After we visited him, he led marches and called for independence through non-violence. And do you remember the guy from Alabama?

PAST: Ugh! We had to visit him in a jail cell.

PRESENT: Yeah, but soon after he, too, was leading marches in Birmingham and even talked about his dream in speeches. You can't say he didn't change any lives for the better.

PAST: OK, I'll admit we've helped our share of men, women, and even children in the past but… it's just… oh, I don't know. Instead of frightening poor people in their sleep and demoralizing them into realizing how worthless they have been in the big scheme of things, couldn't we just spend the holidays relaxing on some tropical beach somewhere?

PRESENT: Oh come on. Tell me you wouldn't miss it–the dramatic appearance out of nowhere, the anticipation, the mystery, the look of utter disbelief and confusion when they first see you.

PAST: It's true. That never gets old.

PRESENT: Exactly. (*to FUTURE*) And you! You get to take it all to a stunning and enthralling conclusion. We set them up for you and then you get to pull back the curtain and reveal to them a most horrifying destiny. How great is that?

> [*FUTURE shakes his/her head up and down but doesn't smile.*]

PAST: (*to PRESENT*) Wow! A smile!

PRESENT: (*to PAST*) You see? You'd miss it all. You'd be sippin' on a mojito, complaining about the bright sunshine, and wishing you were skulking around the cobwebs and cracked corners of someone's darkest dream.

PAST: Maybe.

PRESENT: You just don't want to admit that I might be right.

PAST: Sure. Whatever. But, do you think you're really going to find the next mover and shaker of the world in this crowd? Look at them. It's the holiday season and they've forgotten all their cares. There's no redemption here.

> [*PRESENT gives PAST a cold stare while PAST just shrugs. As they do this, FUTURE slowly raises his/her arm and points a finger at the audience.*]

PAST: (*noticing FUTURE*) Hey! What's up?

PRESENT: What are you talking about?

> [*PAST nods toward FUTURE who is still pointing.*]

PRESENT: (*to FUTURE*) Hey, put your arm down. It's rude to point.

> [*FUTURE lowers his/her arm but continues to point. PAST and PRESENT look toward people in the audience.*]

PRESENT: What? What is it? (*tries to see where FUTURE is pointing*) The woman at the table?

> [*FUTURE shakes a "no."*]

PAST: The drunk guy making a fool of himself with that woman?

> [*FUTURE shakes a "no."*]

PRESENT: (*cranes his neck*) Wait! The young man who just walked in?

> [*FUTURE nods a "yes."*]

PRESENT: (*grimaces*) He's suffering. I can feel it. (*to PAST*) Well?

PAST: (*looks*) Oh, I see him. (*a beat*) He recently lost his job... hasn't found any meaningful work since... his wife is threatening to leave him... with the kids.

PRESENT: But he has a good heart. He wants to do better.

PAST: (*points to FUTURE*) Clearly you already have his/her vote. Can't stop talking about him.

> [*FUTURE is still pointing in the same direction. PRESENT puts his hand over FUTURE's hand and guides it down to the table.*]

PRESENT: Then we're agreed. (*gathers stuff together*) Drink up and let's get going. It's going to be a long night. (*rises from the table and exits*)

PAST: (*to FUTURE*) When are you going to learn to keep your mouth shut? (*rises from the table and exits*)

> [*FUTURE rises slowly from the table and walks forward toward the audience while raising his/her finger and pointing. After several steps, PAST enters*]

and takes FUTURE by the arm and leads him/her off the stage.]

<u>CURTAIN</u>

An Inconvenient Crime

Cast (2M, 1 F)

VINCE - A well-off businessman who dresses and acts conservatively.

ANNETTE - The wife of VINCE. She is more lively than her husband but restrains herself. She also dresses conservatively but with a touch of flair.

BRUCE - A soft-spoken man who dresses cheap but nice.

Scene

The living room of a house. The front door (real or imaginary) is to one side of the room. The room has a few fixtures such as chairs, lamps, and a table with some books and magazines. A variety of knick-knacks can be strewn about. At the fourth wall imagine a roaring fireplace with a large painting above it.

Time

Present.

> *[At rise, VINCE and ANNETTE are each seated in a chair facing the audience at an imaginary fireplace. VINCE is reading a paper while ANNETTE is first texting on then flipping through her phone.]*

ANNETTE: The Horvats went to Europe again.

VINCE: How nice for them.

ANNETTE: They posted pictures of themselves and their dumpy kid in front of the Eiffel Tower. How arrogant.

VINCE: That's what everyone does to show they have the perfect life–online only, of course.

ANNETTE: It's just so annoying.

VINCE: You did the same thing when we went to Rome.

ANNETTE: I took pictures of the old buildings. I wanted to share with everyone the architectural wonders they may not have seen otherwise.

VINCE: I didn't realize your new dress was an architectural wonder.

ANNETTE: Well, I can't be seen at St. Peter's Cathedral in some shabby old sack now can I?

VINCE: When's the last time you wore anything close to a shabby old sack?

ANNETTE: I'm just saying that if you're going to be seen at some thousand-year-old building, you should look your best.

VINCE: Especially if that thousand-year-old building is going to be the backdrop for your online post.

ANNETTE: You just don't understand.

VINCE: Well, you've got that right. I don't.

ANNETTE: You're still reading newspapers. When are you going to update and read online like everyone else?

VINCE: I like newspapers. You can touch them and hold them.

ANNETTE: (*under her breath*) Maybe I should be a newspaper.

VINCE: What was that?

ANNETTE: I said I hope you...

[*There is a knock at the door.*]

VINCE: You expecting anyone?

ANNETTE: Um, no. Are you?

VINCE: Not at this time of the evening. (*a beat*) Maybe they'll go away.

    [There is another knock with more force.]

ANNETTE: Doesn't sound like he's going away. Maybe you should see who it is–might be important.

VINCE: I'd rather just ignore him.

ANNETTE: I think you should see who it is. What if it's someone who needs help?

VINCE: Oh, alright.

    [VINCE sets down his paper and walks to the door.]

VINCE: (*to the door*) Who is it?

    [There is no answer, just another frantic knock on the door. VINCE peers through the peephole.]

VINCE: (*to ANNETTE*) It's just some guy.

ANNETTE: Is he alone?

VINCE: Yes.

ANNETTE: Why don't you see what he wants?

VINCE: Do you have any idea what kind of insane madman could be on the other side of that door? He could be a mass murderer or a mafia hitman.

ANNETTE: Does he LOOK like a mass murderer or a hit man?

VINCE: (*looks through the peephole again*) Well, no. I guess not.

ANNETTE: Well, then, put the chain on, open the door, and at least see what he wants.

VINCE: (*sigh*) Always the bleeding heart.

    [VINCE slides on the door chain and opens the door a few inches.]

VINCE: What do you want?

BRUCE: I'm sorry to bother you, sir, but would you mind if I come in and ask you a question?

VINCE (*upset*) Yes I mind if you come in. I don't know you. You could be some kind of serial killer or something. So, unless you're here to offer me the winning in some kind of million-dollar sweepstakes, go away.

BRUCE: Oh, no sir. It's nothing like that. I have come to ask for your assistance is all.

VINCE: With what?

BRUCE: Please, sir. It's cold out here. Could I just step in for a moment and talk to you?

ANNETTE: What does he want?

VINCE: He says he needs help and wants to come in.

ANNETTE: Then let him in and see what he needs. He might be in trouble or something.

VINCE: Or we could be in trouble.

ANNETTE: What if he is telling the truth and you send him away? How would that make you feel?

VINCE: (*to BRUCE through the door opening*) Go away!

> [*VINCE slams the door shut, walks to his chair, and sits back down.*]

VINCE: It makes me feel just fine, thank you.

ANNETTE: For goodness sake!

> [*ANNETTE puts her phone on a nearby table, gets up, walks to the door, and opens it. BRUCE walks in.*]

VINCE: (*to BRUCE*) OK. You're in. Now, what do you want?

> [*ANNETTE sits back down in her chair.*]

BRUCE: Well, sir, it's just that I noticed you have a very nice house and...

VINCE: You've been casing our house?

BRUCE: Just noticing is all.

VINCE: So what do you want, a photo? You going to feature our house in Better Homes and Gardens?

BRUCE: No, sir. What I would like to do, if it wouldn't be too inconvenient, is to take some of your stuff.

ANNETTE: What?

VINCE: Are you kidding?

BRUCE: If it wouldn't be too much of an inconvenience.

VINCE: Well of course it would be an inconvenience! Did you think we would just let you walk in here and rob us?

BRUCE: Not everything. Just a few things.

VINCE: And that's supposed to make it OK? Just a few things?

BRUCE: Yes, sir. Just a few things is all.

VINCE: Well, that's it! I'm calling the police. (*to ANNETTE*) Give me your phone.

> [*ANNETTE hands VINCE her phone.*]

ANNETTE: (*to VINCE*) Maybe he has a good reason. (*to BRUCE*) Why do you want to rob us?

> [*As BRUCE talks, VINCE can be heard on the phone with the police. At first, he talks calmly but then gets more agitated.*]

BRUCE: It's just that my family has been having a hard time lately. We are behind on our bills and we can't make enough to pay them and keep up with our medications. We can't afford better insurance. We just need a little help to make ends meet.

VINCE: (*on the phone*) No! I'm not making this up. He's here right now. You need to send someone down here right away.

BRUCE: You two look like you are doing very well so I thought maybe I could just come over and take a few things.

ANNETTE: But, mister, uh...

BRUCE: You can just call me Bruce.

ANNETTE: Bruce, don't you think breaking the law would put you in an even worse situation?

BRUCE: No laws will be broken if you give me permission.

ANNETTE: Oh, I see.

VINCENT: (*handing back the phone to ANNETTE*) They didn't believe me but I think I persuaded them to come anyway though they may not be in much of a hurry.

ANNETTE: Bruce here was just saying...

VINCENT: (*to ANNETTE*) Bruce, is it? Now you're on a first name basis?

ANNETTE: He was pointing out the fact that if we let him rob us then he won't be breaking any laws.

VINCENT: LET him rob us? I have no intention of letting him take anything of ours.

BRUCE: Would it be better if I came back next week?

VINCENT: No. It would be better if you didn't come back at all.

BRUCE: You do have insurance on all your belongings, don't you?

VINCENT: (*losing patience*) Of course we have insurance. What business is that of yours? I've had just about enough of you. If you're not out of this house in... (*stops to think*) Wait! What exactly are you saying, uh... Bruce?

BRUCE: Well, you see you wouldn't actually have to lose out. I could take a few things–things maybe that you are tired of or no longer want. Perhaps you want a bigger TV or would like to upgrade to one of those smart refrigerators.

ANNETTE: (*a little over the top*) Oh, now! That's preposterous.

Why would we let you take things just so we could get something bigger and better? I mean that's awfully presumptuous of you. That's a lot of paperwork and time we would have to put in just to get more modern appliances or state-of-the-art technology that could be the envy of the entire neighborhood. I think you should just take your arrogant and rude self out of here before you are arrested for bad ideas.

BRUCE: (*to ANNETTE*) Now hold on there, dear. (*a beat*) He may be on to something. (*a beat*) I mean, maybe we should do our civic duty and help out the less fortunate.

ANNETTE: But you said...

VINCENT: (*to ANNETTE*) Never mind that. (*to BRUCE*) What did you have in mind?

BRUCE: Well, you could give me a list of the things you would like to replace and I'll take them off your hands for you. You report them stolen and get the insurance money to use however you like. When the check comes in you can replace all those things with something better or maybe get something you've always wanted.

VINCENT: Well, why didn't you just say so from the beginning? (*looking around*) Let's see. What can we get rid of?

ANNETTE: We've got a set of dishes in the dining room we've never even used.

VINCENT: Oh sure, yeah and how about that blender you're brother gave us. I don't think we ever took it out of the box.

ANNETTE: (*excited*) How about a new dining room set?

BRUCE: Too big. Hard to move. Electronics always do well, though.

VINCENT: Computers, stereos, tape recorders, that sort of thing?

BRUCE: Maybe not the tape recorders, but, yeah.

VINCENT: Great! I can fill a whole box full of gadgets.

ANNETTE: (*to BRUCE*) Microwave?

BRUCE: Sure.

ANNETTE: Toaster oven?

BRUCE: Absolutely.

VINCENT: Deplorable family portrait with Uncle Ned picking his nose?

BRUCE: Not so much. (*looks toward the painting over the fireplace*) But what about that painting?

VINCENT: (*a little nervous*) Oh, that thing? It's not worth much.

ANNETTE: That's not what you said when you got it.

VINCENT: (*with a fake laugh*) I said it was valuable to me, not that it was actually valuable.

> [BRUCE walks toward the painting and gives it a close look while VINCENT continues to get nervous.]

BRUCE: I wouldn't be so sure. (*a beat*) I've moved quite a few pieces of art in my day. (*looks closer*) The brush strokes, the color, the oils used... This could be authentic.

VINCENT: Oh, come on. It's just a cheap fake. I got it for next to nothing.

ANNETTE: That's not what you...

VINCENT: Look, Bruce. I know the burglary business must keep you busy and that you have a lot to do so we won't keep you. I'll box up all these things for you and then you can come back next week and pick them up.

BRUCE: (*still looking at the painting*) This is exquisite. I would bet anything that this is genuine. (*to VINCENT*) How much did you spend on it?

VINCENT: I, uh, don't remember.

BRUCE: Whatever you paid, it was a bargain.

ANNETTE: But, Vincent. When you brought it home you kept going on about how you got an original Degas painting for a steal.

VINCENT: Oh, come on. I was just joking. You know. It was all a big game. How could I possibly get my hands on a real painting like that?

BRUCE: Because it was stolen.

VINCENT: What?

BRUCE: Looks like one of the pieces taken from the Metropolitan Museum a few years ago? (*turns around to VINCENT*) That's the thing about us thieves. We sometimes tell each other things.

VINCENT: (*suddenly mad*) Alright, that's it! I've had quite enough of your games. You can just leave now before I get really upset.

BRUCE: And what are you going to tell the police when they get here?

VINCENT: The police? The police! They'll be here any minute. (*a beat*) Oh my! I just remembered I have an important meeting down at the office. (*to ANNETTE*) Bye, dear! (*grabs his coat, a briefcase, and exits*)

> [*BRUCE and ANNETTE remain behind and stare at each other for some time. Then, they come together and kiss each other.*]

ANNETTE: You did it!

BRUCE: We did it!

> [*BRUCE and ANNETTE put their arms around each other and slowly exit.*]

BRUCE: When you first told me your idea, I was a little skeptical.

ANNETTE: (*a beat*) Will they catch him?

BRUCE: Every cop in the city will be looking for him and after they catch him, he'll be gone for a long time.

> [*BRUCE and ANNETTE exit.*]

<u>CURTAIN</u>

The Waiting Room

Cast (1 M 1F 2A)

THE FATHER (M) - a man, 40s/50s, wears business clothes.

THE MOTHER (F) - a woman, 40s/50s, married to THE FATHER wearing comfortable clothes.

THE YOUTH (M, F) - a young person, 18-25, who is the son or daughter of THE FATHER and THE MOTHER.

THE CLIENT/THE DRIVER (M, F) - a part that can be played by two people or one person in two roles. THE CLIENT is a business person with a jacket and, possibly, a hat. THE DRIVER is a teenager with a ripped or torn shirt. The same person can play the part by wearing a jacket over the ripped shirt.

Scene

In the front and center is a row of chairs facing the audience. Behind the chairs on stage left is a desk or table with papers on it. Behind the chairs on stage right is another table with two chairs and partially filled glasses.

Time

Present.

> [At rise, THE FATHER sits in the last stage left chair.
> After several long moments of waiting, THE FATHER
> addresses the audience as if just noticing them.]

THE FATHER: (*to the audience*) You new here? (*a beat*) I thought so. Look, I know you're a little confused and uncertain but you need to know it will be alright. (*a beat*) It's not that bad, really. It's comfortable and quiet... maybe a little too quiet I know but you'll get used to it. (*several beats*) You really ought to just sit and relax. It could be quite a long wait.

> [THE FATHER *is seen waiting for several more long moments before addressing the audience again.*]

THE FATHER: It's a quandary, really. I can't wait to see them... my wife and daughter. They will be along but I don't want to rush them either. By all means, they should take their time and enjoy themselves–they deserve that. (*a beat*) It's just that I really do miss them and I can't wait for us to be back together. But... I must wait. That's all there is to it. They are there and I am here. (*a beat*) I am here for them.

> [THE MOTHER *comes on stage left then looks over some papers on the table.*]

THE FATHER: (*to audience*) My wife? She's an investment banker, a real go-getter. She tells me she's in it for people who need help. They need a community bank with friendly people who will help keep the small businesses going because it's the small companies, she says, that help the community: the mom-and-pop grocery stores, the local pharmacy, the mechanic you know by name. They are the ones that sustain the town and its people. (*a beat*) I guess it's how she gets past the office politics, the sexist comments from her male colleagues and insensitive business owners. (*a beat*) It's how she keeps that twinkle in her eye that first caught my attention and caused me to fall in love with her.

> [THE YOUTH *enters stage left and begins a silent conversation with* THE MOTHER.]

THE FATHER: My daughter (*or son*) is much like her mother. She likes to set high goals and then works hard to achieve them. Sometimes she's a bit too hard on herself, though. I think her goals are loftier than they should be and she sets herself up for failure. Just when you think she is about to hit an impenetrable obstacle, though, she breaks through and succeeds but the toll it takes on her can be hard.

> *[As THE FATHER talks, THE CLIENT enters stage*
> *right and sits at the table. He takes a drink.]*

THE FATHER: I took her to parks and movies and we loved to go to lunch together when we had the chance. I'm just afraid she will become like me–driven to the point of blindness where you no longer see why a quiet dinner at home is more important than making the clients happy over drinks.

THE CLIENT: (*looking towards THE FATHER*) Hey! Come join me. Have a drink!

THE FATHER: (*ignores THE CLIENT and continues*) I told my boss I hate those things–those late night office parties; I detest them. You have to act as though you really care about what people are saying when all the time you are thinking about going home to have a nice quiet dinner with your family before watching TV and going to bed. It's all a game. You don't really care about the clients and they don't really care about you and everyone knows it but we just keep pretending that we are all having a good time. Then, at some point between the desert and the final cocktail, a small deal is struck. The clients are happy, the company is happy, everyone has another drink.

THE CLIENT: C'mon, man! The drinks are cold and the women are hot!

> *[THE FATHER joins THE CLIENT at the table*
> *and picks up the other glass but does not drink.*
> *He and THE CLIENT have a mock conversation*
> *peppered with pompous and fake laughter between*
> *them. After a few moments, THE FATHER faces the*
> *audience while THE CLIENT continues to silently*
> *laugh and carry on with THE FATHER as if he was*
> *still in the same position.]*

THE FATHER: (*to the audience*) I don't drink. I don't like alcohol. It turns people into maddening fools. Maybe that's why I hate these things–not only are you expected to be away from your family with a bunch of insincere con artists but you are supposed to drink heavily until you can belt out your deepest prejudices and arrogant conceits and blame it on the booze if anyone seems offended.

> [*THE CLIENT waves goodbye and exits with his drink. THE FATHER pats him on the back and then returns to his seat on the bench with his own drink.*]

THE FATHER: I get one drink and I nurse it all night. Sometimes I slip in another ice cube when no one is looking until, by the end of the night, the glass is filled mostly with water. (*puts his drink down*) I always feared being the person you hear about the next morning–the one who was so drunk he crossed over the meridian late at night and smashed into an oncoming vehicle. (*a beat*) But sometimes accidents happen anyway. Even if you are the most careful person in the world, even if you barely drink, even if you follow all the rules of the road and do what your parents taught you to do when you drive a car late at night, accidents still happen. Sometimes you are the drunken fool veering haplessly across the line and sometimes you are the unfortunate person on the other side of that line.

> [*As THE FATHER talks, THE DRIVER walks onstage looking confused and sits in the last stage right chair.*]

THE DRIVER: (*looks around*) Where am I? (*a beat*) What am I doing here?

THE FATHER: (*speaks softly but does not look at THE DRIVER*) Waiting.

THE DRIVER: (*looks at THE FATHER*) What?

THE FATHER: (*looks into the far distance*) You must wait.

THE DRIVER: Wait? Wait for what?

THE FATHER: For those you left behind.

THE DRIVER: (*panicked*) No! I'm not staying here. I have to get back.

THE FATHER: You can't. (*a beat*) All you can do is wait... Wait and remember.

> [*THE DRIVER looks around desperately then realizes he has nowhere to go. He sits down dejected. THE MOTHER enters stage left. She walks to the desk and begins shuffling through the papers. She seems very distressed.*]

THE MOTHER: (*to offstage*) Have you seen my flashlight?

THE YOUTH: (*from offstage*) What?

THE MOTHER: My flashlight, my flashlight! Have you seen it?

THE YOUTH: (*walking onstage*) Isn't it in the desk drawer?

THE MOTHER: (*still searching*) I've looked and I can't find it anywhere.

THE YOUTH: It might be in the kitchen. I was about to make some coffee. I'll see if I can find it. (*starts to leave*)

> [*THE MOTHER gets frustrated with looking then starts to cry. THE YOUTH turns to her.*]

THE YOUTH: Oh, mother... (she moves toward THE MOTHER)

THE MOTHER: (*slams down the papers on the desk*) Oh, why did he have to go to that party?

THE YOUTH: (*taking THE MOTHER in her arms*) I don't know.

THE MOTHER: Couldn't he have said no? Just this once? He could have!

THE YOUTH: I know, mom. I guess he felt he had to. Here, let's look again for that flashlight. (*searches then finds the flashlight*) Here it is.

THE MOTHER: Oh, thank you. I have to go down to the basement to look for some documents and I think a fuse is out.

THE DAUGHTER: Would you like me to go with you? I think there's another flashlight in the kitchen.

THE MOTHER: (*drying her eyes*) Yes, please. I hate going down there in the dark.

> [*THE MOTHER and THE YOUTH exit the stage. As they do, the stage lights go down. THE DRIVER begins to cry.*]

THE FATHER: (*still in the dark*) I remember when I cried like that. It was just a few months after my little brother's accident. My dad said it was time to be strong and to stop crying but I couldn't stop. I loved my little brother. They said the pain would eventually go away and that I would stop hurting but every day that he was not there was just as painful as the last. I tried to be brave. I just whimpered and hoped that no one would hear me. I didn't want anyone to know that I thought of that moment every day–the day my little brother was taken by a truck–ripped away from his seat while the rest of us just watched in horror. I couldn't understand why he was taken and not me. I thought it should have been me. It SHOULD have been me.

> [*From offstage, THE MOTHER and THE YOUTH flip on their flashlights and point them to the back of the stage. They walk onstage and direct their beams to circle around from the back until they are pointed toward THE FATHER as he talks.*]

THE DRIVER: Who's out there? Is anyone out there?

THE FATHER: Usually when you drive late at night you are only vaguely aware of the streams of white lights that pass by to your left. Like a pair of low flying jets they appear in the distance and glide past you smoothly and evenly but the lights I had noticed on the edge of my consciousness were darting about as if they were searching for someone. (*a beat*) By the time I realized that those lights had sought me out and were headed right for me, it was too late for me to react in any useful way. Like the hapless deer in an open field, the bright lights captured me and froze me into a state of fear that made it impossible to respond. The lights blinded me for a moment until they shot heavenward and I saw the undercarriage of the car. Like a cannonball, the car shot upward over the median strip and then descended directly toward me. The whole event took no more than a few seconds but I remember every single part of those few seconds and, to me, the time slowed until I could see the events of every microsecond as if they were separate frames in a movie. When the front of the car came toward me, I could see how my headlights briefly penetrated the cab of the car coming at me. It was then that I saw her (his) face. She was young and afraid. Her eyes were heavy like she was exhausted or maybe she had been drinking. Her hands clutched the steering until they were whiter than ghosts and I imagined her foot was pushing the brake in a futile attempt to stop what was happening.

> *[THE DRIVER screams. The lights come up. Both THE DRIVER and THE FATHER stare forward.]*

THE YOUTH: Fixed the fuse. (*switches off flashlight*)

THE MOTHER: (*switches off flashlight*) Oh, thank you. (*she looks around and see the papers on the stage right table*) There they are.

> *[THE MOTHER takes some papers and looks over them then begins sobbing. THE YOUTH goes to THE MOTHER and puts arm around her and helps her exit stage right.]*

THE DRIVER: (*still facing forward*) I... uh... I'm sorry. (*pauses then turns very slowly towards THE FATHER*) I'm so sorry.

> *[THE FATHER stares ahead for a moment then slowly turns toward THE DRIVER. He begins to recognize him/her. First, he is confused then he becomes angry. He begins to say something then stops himself. He calms down.]*

THE FATHER: (*to THE DRIVER*) It's all right. It's all right now.

Everything will be alright.

[As THE DRIVER talks, THE FATHER rises from his seat and stands next to it.]

THE DRIVER: (*looks forward*) I'm new here (*a beat*) Confused and uncertain but I think... I hope it will be alright. (*a beat*) It's comfortable and quiet–maybe a little too quiet–but I'll get used to it.... I'll get used to it. (*looks down*) I'll get used to the waiting.

THE FATHER: (*to the audience*) I remember when I first came here. I remember when I saw him sitting there. (*motions to the seat where he was just sitting*) He was exactly how I remembered him. He was young and vibrant and looked at me with that smile that always made me feel so good. He was just how I remembered him before the accident. (*pauses to look toward the seat*) I remember his face. It was a face of understanding and peace. It was a young face filled with ancient wisdom. (*turns back to the audience*) He told me he had been waiting... waiting for me and that he was fine. He told me that I would be fine. Everything will be alright, he said. Then, he hugged me with those little arms and I felt waves of love, peace, and beauty surround me. It was in the midst of that embrace that I understood it all. I knew why I had to wait. He was right, of course: everything would be all right. I watched him look at me before he walked away and disappeared but I knew he would always be with me in my heart. He had waited here for me. Now it's my turn to wait. (*sits back down in the seat*) So, I wait.

[The lights slowly fade.]

<u>Curtain</u>

About The Author

Kenneth P. Langer

Rev. Dr. Kenneth P. Langer is an ordained Universalist minister and a former college professor with graduate degrees in both music and theology. He is a published writer, composer, and poet and is the author of several works of fiction as well as books on spiritual living. He also enjoys playing and designing games.

Learn more by visiting his website: http://kennethplanger.com

Books In This Series

Ten Minute Plays
Collections of original ten-minute plays

Ten By Ten Book One

Characters search for a conflict, upset audience members disrupt the show, a spy mission goes wrong, cowboys try but can't do a simple shootout correctly, and a considerate and mannerly thief asks permission before he robs people. These are some of the situations found in this collection of ten-minute plays. Here are delightful theatrical nuggets that range from the comical to the serious. Each one is designed to be produced with just a few actors, few props, and within a single setting. They are easy to perform or fun to just read.

Ten By Ten Book Two

Stagehands argue about their relationship between acts, a mountain climber struggles to rise above the summit of public opinion, the man once sent to kill a princess finds her working at a diner, retired superheroes lament their new life, and a villain threatens to blow up the world if he can get the Henchman Union to end contract negotiations. These are some of the situations found in this second collection of ten-minute plays. Each one is designed to be produced with just a few actors, few props, and within a single setting. They are easy to perform or fun to just read.

Ten By Ten Book Three

An interstellar Do Not Disturb sign, a smartwatch that may be a little too smart, love found in a silent meditation retreat, two former circus clowns enter a boxing ring, and an entire conversation with only three words are just some of the humorous and dramatic situations found in this third collection of ten-minute plays. Each one is designed to be produced with just a few actors, a few props, and within one or two simple settings. They are easy to perform or fun to just read.

Ten By Ten Book Four

An undercover vampire, a prophetic park bench, an audience on stage, a mixed-up fairy tale, a bad hand, a little gibberish, some self care, a dental obsession, and the end of the world are some of the things you will encounter in this fourth collection of ten-minute plays. Most are designed to be produced with just a few actors, a few props, and within one or two simple settings. They are easy to perform or fun to just read.

Other Books

Non-Fiction

- Spirituality
  - A Different Calling: A Manual for Lay Ministers and Other Non-Professional Facilitators of Any Spiritual Tradition
  - Many Leaves, One Tree: A Collection of Aphorisms Inspired by the Tao Te Ching
  - The Purpose Derived Life: What In The Universe Am I Here For?
  - Three Guidelines for Ethical Living
  - Playing Cards and the Game of Living Well
  - The Emergence of God: The Intersection of Science, Nature, and Spirituality
  - The Langer Deck
  - Emergent Spirituality: Principles and Practices at the Intersection of Science, Nature, and Spirituality
  - Open Hearts and Open Doors: Radical Hospitality in the Church
  - Let Us Wander: A Ministry of Music and Arts
- Games
  - 52 New Card Games (For Those Old Cards)
  - 36 New Dice Games
  - 40 Games for Forty Dice
  - Castle Imbroglio: An Escape Adventure Book
- Music
  - A Guide to the Art of Musical Performance
  - A Theory for All Music

- Book 1: Fundamentals
- Book 2: Chords and Part-Writing
- Book 3: The Tools of Analysis
- Book 4: Parametric Analysis
- Rounds and Canons for Peace and Justice
- Music for Unitarian-Universalist Choirs
- Songs of Worship
- 50 Songs for Meditation

Fiction

- Science Fiction
  - The Milleran Cluster Series
    - Of Eternal Light
    - The Forever Horizon
    - The Suicide Fire
    - The Song of the Mother
    - The Journey of Awri
- Theater
  - Four Comedies
  - 10 x 10: Ten Ten-Minute Plays Book 1
  - 10 x 10: Ten Ten-Minute Plays Book 2
  - 10 x 10: Ten Ten-Minute Plays Book 3
  - 10 x 10: Ten Ten-Minute Plays Book 4
  - Ageless Wisdom: Multigenerational Plays for Worship
- Poetry
  - Looking At The World: A Collection of Poetry
  - Prayers

Final Note

Thank you for reading this book!

If you enjoyed reading it please let me know
and please consider writing a positive online review.

Ken Langer

Contact Information
personal website: http://kennethplanger.com
book site: http://brassbellbooks.com
Email: klangerdude@gmail.com